State Capitalism and World Revolution

C.L.R. James
Written in Collaboration
with Raya Dunayevskaya
and Grace Lee Boggs

State Capitalism and World Revolution
C.L.R. James, Raya Dunayevskaya, and Grace Lee Boggs

This edition © PM Press 2013

PM Press
PO Box 23912
Oakland, CA 94623
www.pmpress.org

Published in conjunction with the Charles H. Kerr Publishing Company
C.H. Kerr Company
1726 Jarvis Avenue
Chicago, IL 60626
www.charleshkerr.com

Cover design by Josh MacPhee/justseeds.org/antumbradesign.org
Layout by Jonathan Rowland

ISBN: 978-1-60486-092-4
LCCN: 2012913639

10 9 8 7 6 5 4 3 2

Printed in the USA.

Contents

A Note to the 2013 Edition

TIMES HAVE CHANGED and changed again (one could easily say, again and again and again) since the original publication of this unique document in 1950. As I explain below in the Introduction to the 1986 Edition—written only a few years before I took up the task of writing the authorized biography of C.L.R. James, and James himself passed away—the principal author had moved from obscurity to celebrity during the 1970s. By the time of the 1986 edition, he was the *éminence grise* of Pan-Africanism, because he had outlived his generation, but mainly because he was an infinitely wise—to the casual look also infinitely aged—world historic revolutionary.

Capitalism, globally centered in the American empire, regained its strength and self-confidence by the early 1950s, then lost much of what it had gained by 1970. The Marxist analysis that James and his collaborators had laid out then appeared vindicated, with the demographic changes in the workforce bringing layers of women and nonwhites into production and distribution. But deindustrialization was only around the corner. The triumphant capitalism of the 1990s, basking in the warmth of the East Bloc collapse but also in the money-gush of financialized economies, would seem to have wiped the theories and implied strategies of *State Capitalism and World Revolution* off the map. State capitalism as a system had indeed spun downward in its own contradictions, but corporate capitalism was the apparent victor, with the spoils going to new classes of exploiters. Only China, more "capitalist" in its state capitalism than ever before, remained vital, an obstacle but also partner to an all-out triumph called the "End of History," that is, the history of class struggle. That was, of course, a superficial and self-interested reading of the situation.

What would C.L.R. James have made of the failed imperial wars in Iraq and Afghanistan, the implosion of the finance-capital economy, and the election of a nonwhite U.S. president presiding over the deeply troubled empire? We may be sure that he would have insisted upon the inevitability of the economic and social contradictions, and would have responded eagerly to Occupy, as the voice of the voiceless, come onto the stage of history to be heard. It was in his nature—and so unlike many a would-be Marxist savant—to look for what was new, what fresh stream of activity caught public attention and encouraged bursts of rebellious activity along new lines.

James wrote the remarkable foreword to the 1986 edition against the background of the Solidarity movement's triumph in Poland. It bespoke an optimism that carried over in many places, especially East Germany, with the fall of the Communist regimes, that something better, more tied to working class life and collective self-determination, was possible, if not certain. That hope disappeared rather quickly, although not without leaving behind new formations symptomized by the appearance of the Left Party in Germany, during the era to follow. More to the point, in some ways, the vast Communist Party entourage in Italy, for a time the largest political party of any kind in Europe, all but dissolved in the aftermath of the East Bloc debacle. It became clear that the Communist following had been mainly old-time faithful, and with their passing went the factories they had worked in since the Second World War, and the basis for the European Left. So little seemed to be left behind at the dawn of a new century.

The same was true, of course, for European socialist parties, more subservient than any but the most cynical observer could have predicted to the new austerity programs and the steady rollback of social safety nets, victories in lowering the retirement age, and so on. The successes of the social democratic struggles in modifying and even creating a particular state capitalism were now at an end.

And yet the importance of the history of the working class as a global phenomenon remained, and not only because a vast new working class had emerged in China and begun to struggle for collective self-recognition. How had the vast Left movements of the twentieth century run aground? What in Marxist writings helped explain successes and failures, especially the storied triumph of revolution in Russia, and its retreat? *State Capitalism and World Revolution* remains a vital read, if not necessarily an easy one. And C.L.R. James, in this writing as perhaps nowhere else (except *The Black Jacobins* and *Beyond a Boundary*) reveals what he has to say to the future.

Paul Buhle
Madison, Wisconsin, April 2012

Fully and Absolutely Assured
(C.L.R. James' Foreword to the 1986 Edition)

THIRTY YEARS AGO those who adhered to revolutionary Marxism or who thought about it were in ferment. Dominating the discussion were the views of Trotsky, who was universally looked upon as continuing the Marx, Engels and Lenin tradition. In fact Trotsky's name was used most often in association with Lenin. Lenin and Trotsky summed up the official Marxist position of the day.

The importance of *State Capitalism and World Revolution*, published in 1950, was that it not only projected a theory of state capitalism, but at its very beginning it stated definitely and unequivocally that Trotsky's whole method of analysis and results were to be repudiated. As I look back at the appearance of this document and those days, I am frequently reminded of the fact that some of the people in the United States who read it were not so much impressed at the beginning with the theory of state capitalism: They were startled and, in fact, bewildered at the fact that I had challenged directly the Marxist ideas of Lenin and Trotsky (as they thought it)—the Trotsky who had led the October Revolution to victory.

The power of the Johnson-Forest Tendency, which led them to challenge with such effrontery the leader of the Third International and the initiator of the Fourth, was the last writings of Lenin. Today, thirty years after this document *State Capitalism and World Revolution* was produced, the writings of Lenin, particularly in his last days, still remain the foundation of any attempt to observe, to organize, to assist in any way the movement toward Marxism—that is to say toward the emancipation of the working class.

That last phrase sounds awkward in my ears today. Today I do not know of any body of people who speak or preach with any confidence of the "emancipation of the working class." People are not against, not at all—but they are not for. Political thought in relation to society at this most critical period in human history is in a state of suspended animation. That is not quite true. There is no animation, but there is not stagnation. There is a conscious desire to wait and see.

In Poland in 1981, the working class and the people of Poland registered the first basis of the new conception of the emancipation of the working class. The people of Poland formed a socialist party—but this was a party to end all parties. It consisted of ten million Polish people. In fact the able-bodied people of Poland, the men and women, formed a party which did not represent the people, but itself consisted of the people. The people were the party and the party was the people.

I do not think that I should here go into the ideas which are sufficiently expounded and bear up against all the problems of the day, in the document *State Capitalism and World Revolution*. However, for me Marxism is itself the movement of history and I cannot do better than to make clear that what the reader will find in this document is a restatement in contemporary terms of Lenin's most profound reflections in 1923 as he knew he was dying and wanted to leave the heritage of the experience to the party, the Russian people and the world revolution. The articles which really matter are: "On Cooperation" (January 4, 1923), again "On Cooperation" (January 6, 1923), "How We Should Reorganize the Workers' and Peasants' Inspection" (January 23, 1923) and "Better Fewer, but Better" (March 2, 1923). I think he was unable to write part of these last articles and had to dictate them. I wish to say only that in those articles he condemned absolutely, in language I have not seen or heard anywhere else, the USSR.

The historical parallel that he made was a bureaucratic organization of society with the mass of the population as serfs that had not yet reached the feudal system in its maturity.

I want to correct or, strictly speaking, indulge myself and state some of the terms he used—*pre-feudal* for the state and *bureaucratic-serf* culture for the people. I may appear to be militant to the point of ferocity. I am because these most important writings, the summation of the greatest political experience the world has ever had, the formation of the Bolshevik Party and the creation of the first Workers' State—this summation is entirely neglected and, I am now convinced, not by any chance. My experience is the people on the Left and generally anti-capitalists, are afraid of it.

I shall now conclude by stating what they are afraid of. Here is Lenin's summation that he entitles *Explanatory Notes*:

> The Soviets are a new state apparatus, which, in the first place, provides an armed force of workers and peasants; and this force is not divorced from the people, as was the old standing army, but is fused with the people in the closest possible fashion. From a military point of view, this force is incomparably more powerful than previous forces; from the point of view of the revolution it cannot be replaced by anything else.
>
> Secondly, this apparatus provides a bond with the masses, with the majority of the people, so intimate, so indissoluble, so readily controllable and renewable, that there was nothing remotely like it in the previous state apparatus.
>
> Thirdly, this apparatus, by virtue of the fact that it is elected and subject to recall at the will of the people without any bureaucratic formalities, is far more democratic than any previous apparatus.
>
> Fourthly, it provides a close contact with the most diverse occupations, thus facilitating the adoption of the most varied and most radical reforms without a bureaucracy,
>
> Fifthly, it provides a form of organization of the vanguard, i.e., of the most class-conscious, most energetic and most progressive section of the oppressed classes, the workers and peasants, and thus constitutes an apparatus with the help of which the vanguard of the oppressed classes can elevate, educate and lead the gigantic masses of these classes, which hitherto have stood remote from political life and from history.
>
> Sixthly, it provides the possibility of combining the advantages of parliamentarism with the advantages of immediate and direct democracy, i.e., of uniting in the persons of the elected representatives of the people both legislative and executive functions. Compared with bourgeois parliamentarism, this represents an advance in the

development of democracy which is of historical and worldwide significance.[1]

There is one aspect of Lenin which cannot be omitted in what I believe was the very last article, "Better Fewer, but Better" (March 1923). Near the end, after outlining the prospects of the world revolution, he concludes:

> In the last analysis, the outcome of the struggle will be determined by the fact that Russia, India, China, etc., account for the overwhelming majority of the population of the globe. And during the past few years it is this majority that has been drawn into the struggle for emancipation with extraordinary rapidity, so that in this respect there cannot be the slightest doubt what the final outcome of the world struggle will be. In this sense, the complete victory of socialism is fully and absolutely assured.[2]

April 9, 1984
London

---

1   V.I. Lenin, *Selected Works*, Vol. VIII, 454.
2   Ibid., Vol. III, 785.

Introduction to the Fourth Edition
(1986)

Two generations ago, C.L.R. James and a small circle of collaborators set forth a revolutionary critique of industrial civilization. Their vision possessed a striking originality. So insular was the political context of their theoretical breakthroughs, however, and so thoroughly did their optimistic expectations for working class activity defy trends away from class and social issues to the so-called "End of Ideology," that the documents of the signal effort never reached public view.

Happily, times have changed. James has become a late-life celebrity, near-legendary *éminence grise* of Pan-Africanism, admired cultural critic. The corpus of his theoretical work is available in three volumes of selected essays; a philosophical work, *Notes on Dialectics*; and his major work of literary criticism, *Mariners, Renegades and Castaways*. Readers have discovered much, even after all these years, to challenge Marxist (or any other) orthodoxy. They will never find a more succinct version of James' general conclusions than *State Capitalism and World Revolution.*[1]

In this slim volume, James and his comrades successfully predict the future course of Marxism. Contrary to reigning Old Left dogmas, they argue that workers on both sides of the Iron Curtain and under any variety of state or private ownership face the same essential contradictions. The drive for ever-expanding productivity disguises a mad rationalism, unable any longer to reconcile its aim of total control with the technological means at hand. This sorcerer's apprentice recognizes

---

1   U.S. editions cited, where available: *The Future in the Present: Selected Essays, Volume I* (Westport, CT: Lawrence Hill, 1977); *Spheres of Existence: Selected Writings, Volume II* (Westport, CT: Lawrence Hill, 1980); *At the Rendezvous of Victory: Selected Essays, Volume III* (London: Alison & Busby, 1984); *Notes on Dialectics* (Westport, CT: Lawrence Hill, 1980); *Beyond a Boundary* (New York: Pantheon Books, 1984).

no democratic, human solution. Socialists, Communists and Trotskyists alike—themselves heir to the ideology of economic fatalism and political elites—tragically share the same blind spot. The old forms of working class expression, such as Left or labor parties, unions and state ownership of production, have become part of the logic of continued capitalist development. New forms of mass self-expression must arise against these bureaucratized institutions and against the assumptions they harbor. Radicals who fail to heed these warnings, to aid the newer developments, betray their own best instincts and the best traditions of Marxism.

The insight expressed here takes us from the world of Trotsky, Stalin and Norman Thomas to the world of New Left, Black Power and Polish Solidarity. But the *form* of argumentation in *State Capitalism and World Revolution* threatens to obscure the actual breakthrough from the casual reader. As James would recall in his autobiographical notes, "the thing that mattered chiefly was the correct political line that had enabled Lenin to defeat all his rivals and to lead the Russian Revolution to success." If this project had been, in retrospect, "a complete illusion," then "we believed in it completely and were able to examine it and find the weaknesses that were in it."[2] From the first lines of the original introduction, the text bristles with manifestations of the immanent critique, attacks on Trotskyist groups and on perspectives unknown outside the small movement. *State Capitalism and World Revolution* must be seen as an exercise in self-clarity or it will not likely be seen at all.

Even the omissions we would now regard as major take on a distinct meaning in this light. The book seems oblivious to ethnicity and religion, always central to working class life, and even to race, an area where James had previously made fundamental contributions. Atomic armament and the struggle against it, the "Woman Question" that had re-emerged sharply during the Second World War and would shortly become a central theoretical issue for James' group—these issues, too, were put aside. Culture, the keynote of social movements since the early 1960s, can hardly be found at all. An almost syndicalist intensity on the shop-floor struggle and its implications crowds out these other issues.

2   From unpublished notes for autobiography, in author's possession.

Only the workers, their essential similarity and potential worldwide links, come fully into view. And that is surely the point. James had to narrow the focus so that the outlines would become clear.

The careful reader will also find a "hidden text" straining to escape the straitjacket of formal political discourse. James and his circle wished to restore the revolutionary continuity of Hegel, the young Marx and the aging Lenin not only for the sake of political strategy, but to recover a conception practically lost since the First International. The founding father of Marxism premised his vision of Socialism upon the abolition of the growing dichotomy between mental and manual labor, a dichotomy which mutilated the worker's natural creativity and which rendered the intellectual an isolate. Lenin, the political chief of an unwanted bureaucratic state apparatus, staged his final struggle to create the basis for direct economic democracy. On anything less than a world scale, the contradictions could not (and cannot) be finally overcome. The age of dictators in the political Kremlins, military Pentagons and state planning bureaus or corporate headquarters had, by the 1940s, seemingly vanquished humanity's best hopes, and relegated "Socialism" to varieties of state regulation. *State Capitalism and World Revolution* insists, rather, that the very heightening of internal antagonisms and catastrophic possibilities means the real end of class society may be closer than the radicals themselves realize. Ordinary people have been prepared by their own uniquely modern experiences, good and bad. Now only the opportunity for the full use of their collective genius is lacking. Couched in the language of political warfare, *State Capitalism and World Revolution* is a gospel of hope. However unrealized that hope thirty-five years later, it remains the alternative to the spread of gulags and bloodbaths, and to the fast-approaching Doomsday.

C.L.R. James' first "American Years," 1938–53, of which this book offers the foremost political evidence, can be seen best as a slice of life surrounded by what had gone before and what has followed. At thirty-one, in 1932, James left his native Trinidad to explore the sources of his British colonial legacy. In the following six years, he managed to become cricket correspondent for the *Manchester Guardian*, a prominent Trotskyist writer and orator, a pioneer of African emancipation and an author of several important books, including the classic history *Black Jacobins* and a Trotskyist "bible" of Comintern history, *World Revolution*

1917–1936. He then exited for America, where he made his home for fifteen years, until his deportation in 1953 (nominally for a passport violation, but in reality because of his political status). Since then James has lived for periods in England, the Caribbean and (after 1970) again in the United States. He has served, into old age, as vigorous radical social theorist, dynamic lecturer, political influence and at times political leader on several continents.[3]

Only in the first American years, however, did James lead a political group for a sustained period, and set out with others to solve, collectively, the puzzle of Marxism's legacy for the late twentieth century. Illuminating this heretofore little-known period of his life offers a way to understand otherwise curious aspects of *State Capitalism and World Revolution*.

The story begins in Coyoacán, Mexico, with James' spirited dialogue with Leon Trotsky. Supported by small if energetic groups, outmaneuvered by the Popular Front coalition which threw vast liberal and social-democratic influences behind Moscow's anti-Fascist policies, Trotsky gamely outlined his plans for a revolutionary breakthrough. James presented a new element in the equation. Virtually Trotskyism's only internationally known Third World figure, James had proved himself in Britain, but as political ally more than disciple. Indeed, James' intellectual and political methods, his wide range of associates in non-political and even Communist milieux had already disturbed British Trotskyist orthodoxy. He would in America shortly join a crusade against Trotsky's leadership and later turn against Trotskyism altogether.

The discussion pitted the two remarkable figures as equals—perhaps to Trotsky's surprise. The obvious bone of contention lay in the "Negro Question" and its larger significance. Trotsky argued in good Bolshevik fashion that blacks would be brought into the Trotskyist party (or into Trotskyist-led mass movements), taught proper politics, and directed the way the Bolsheviks had directed national minorities within and alongside Russian borders. James disputed the contention. Blacks, he insisted, did not need to be led by the labor movement or anyone else. They could be significantly aided by revolutionary thinkers and activists,

---

3   Biographical data from various essays in *C.L.R. James: His Life and Work*, edited by Paul Buhle (London: Allison & Busby, 1986) originally published in *Urgent Tasks* 12 (1981) and *Race Today* (1986).

Introduction to the Fourth Edition

but rather than socialist politics freeing blacks, blacks would themselves precipitate the radical movement in the United States, creating a mass force led by blacks struggling for their democratic rights.[4]

Too much might be made of this particular argument. The great exile gave ground, while most Trotskyists remained fixed in their task of organizing disciplined parties to the exclusion of almost everything else. Trotsky and James shared, after all, a concrete experience in the international arena where political mobilization assumed a variety of different forms.[5] Like the lesser Trotskyists, the two identified the Russian Revolution as the key event of the century and the formation of strong national organizations as chief means to resurrect true internationalism. But James venerated a different Lenin, perhaps, than Trotsky or the Trotskyists. His was a prophet of colonial revolution by people of color, people whose circumstances practically excluded the kind of straightforward proletarian party typical of Europe and much desired in the United States. Implicit in the distinction was also James' confidence in the rural workers on whose backs capitalism accrued its first "primitive accumulation." Their appearance on the stage of history, in their own name, marked not only an economic-social but also a *cultural* turning point in revolutionary possibilities.

"Trotsky declared that the proletariat does not grow under world capitalism and declines in culture. This is absolutely false," James would write in 1950. What he had observed on the cricket fields and calypso tents, he quickly appreciated in Afro-American culture from church rituals to the Cotton Club. The confluence of formerly rural cultures into the industrial-urban proletariat supplied a key to the enigma—although James would not yet phrase it this way—which found Euro-American Marxism at a loss since the First World War and the isolation of the Russian experiment.[6]

---

4   The text of the conversation, but only as regards the first point, is contained in *Leon Trotsky on Black Nationalism and Self-Determination* (New York: Pathfinder Press, 1967).

5   On this and several other points as regards Trotskyism, I wish to thank Kent Worcester for his serious James scholarship and his comradely criticisms.

6   On this point, see especially Sylvia Wynter, "In Quest of Matthew Bondsman: Some Cultural Notes on the Jamesian Journey," in *Urgent Tasks* 12 and *C.L.R. James: His Life and Work*.

James wholeheartedly agreed with Trotsky's goal of forging an "American Bolshevism," but sought a Bolshevism the Trotskyists never anticipated. At Coyoacán, James asked Trotsky why European Trotskyist groups could actually stagnate at a time of rising European labor struggles. He viewed Trotsky's defense of the vanguard party's "ultimate" triumph with considerable skepticism. This disagreement went to the heart of things. The disproportion of Trotskyist vanguard claims and actual influence defied credulity. In other parts of the world where Communists assumed control of the anti-Fascist partisan military forces, their organizations would indeed come to power (purging their radical, democratic critics in the process). But in the unconquered nations and most clearly the United States, the Marxist political parties in their classic form and with their political rather than military aims had by the late 1930s reached the apex of their influence, a rarefied altitude from which descent would be both swift and permanent.

James' observation of American life reinforced this understanding. The self-possession of the ordinary American struck him as almost unbelievable. "Every American citizen, ignorant of so many things that his European counterpart knows, is conscious of himself as a distinct personality, in his own opinion and the opinion of his fellows, as entitled to special consideration of his ideas, his feelings, his likes and dislikes as the most aristocratic heroine of a European novel," James would say in *Mariners, Renegades and Castaways*. But this advance was not painless. Quite to the contrary, for "at the same time, he is consumed by the need of intimate communion with his fellows."[7] Liberation from the weight of the past which holds back Europeans, impels Americans to become free—to grapple urgently for social relations which can turn the universal sense of desperation into an integrated modern self. That could be achieved only by social transformation of a scale and quality considered a distant *successor* to proletarian revolution by nineteenth century Marxists.

Such a view of Socialism, sophisticated even now, was in the 1930s and '40s rare indeed. Similar notions advanced by the anarcho-mystic Gustav Landauer or Lenin's "Ultra-Left" opponent, Dutch poet Herman Gorter, had been outside the main currents of the Left. Some cultural

---

7 "Preface," *Mariners, Renegades and Castaways*.

movements, Surrealism in particular, sought to return questions of consciousness and individual transformation to the center of the revolutionary stage; but these were isolated by the success of Communist machinations and by the shroud of pessimism held above the 1930s movement after the Nazi seizure of power.[8] In the United States, cultural questions remained the province of intellectuals, save in the restricted foreign-language circles of autodidact workers. Actual factory-based movements largely continued an old-fashioned belief in economism, anticipating that the victory of "rational" socialism over "irrational" capitalism would bring automatic solutions to all remaining social problems.

James readily appreciated his exceptional point of observation within American society and sought to make the most of his opportunity for a fresh view free of the familiar Leftist blinders. While taking part in the Trotskyist movement, as lecturer and organizer of Missouri sharecroppers and factional wrangler, he also led a separate and almost "unpolitical" existence. He lived near Harlem and held discussions with intellectuals ranging from Richard Wright to Theodor Adorno. He gulped down American literature, not excepting the "reactionary" Poe and Faulkner. And he struck many of his political associates not only as a brilliant and encyclopedic Marxist thinker but also as an extreme eccentric. Future luminaries from the same circle, such as Irving Howe or Hal Draper, seemed genuinely baffled by his charismatic appeal and by his heterodox views. Others regarded him as mystic, cryptoanarchist or black nationalist.[9]

Probably only a small circle *could* accept perspectives so radically out of kilter with existing doctrines. As James tells the story, the break of a Trotskyist faction with Trotsky himself in 1940 over their unwillingness to support Russia in the coming world war unleashed a profound sense of discontinuity in Marxist tradition. James Burnham, perhaps the most prominent intellectual besides C.L.R. James in the group, unleashed a blistering polemic against dialectical materialism as outdated nonsense disregarded by all serious scientific thought. The faction's

---

8   See, e.g., André Breton: *What Is Surrealism?*, edited by Franklin Rosemont (New York: Monad Press, 1978).

9   Communications from Irving Howe and Hal Draper to the author, discussions with Socialist Workers Party and Workers Party veterans (some in files of the Oral History of the American Left Collection, Tamiment Library, New York University).

main leader, Max Shachtman, propounded a theory of Russian social dynamics which seemed to place the new bureaucratic system outside the Marxist analysis of class contradictions. The roof seemed to be caving in from several directions at once. (Nor was this a misperception. Burnham was, by the late 1940s, the foremost intellectual advocate for military confrontation with the Soviet Union, and Shachtman the policy architect of later AFL-CIO support for the Vietnam War.) James himself wondered if he should return to Britain.

The singular Raya Dunayevskaya, Russian-born intellectual and secretary to Trotsky, persuaded James to stay, in order to begin the collective effort required to renew the basis of Marxist thought. Fluent in Russian, she had already determined that everything Lenin wrote about Marxism, especially his analysis of capitalist production and his commentaries on Marx's relevant interpretations, should be translated and circulated for discussion. Grace Lee, daughter of a prominent Asian-American restaurateur and herself a philosophy PhD, made the pair a trio with her work on German-language materials. (Strange as it now seems, the first English translations from Marx's *1844 Economic-Philosophical Manuscripts* were mimeographed by James' group for discussions with Detroit auto workers.) James supplied the world-view and literary skills for the collective tasks. Around the three grew a following which numbered at its peak around seventy, including union militants, a few black activists, and a direct descendent of Tom Paine.[10]

Only in recent years have historians taken seriously the levels of contemporary discontent which gave James' group spheres of actual influence and reasons to hope for dramatic social change. Wartime strikers rebelled at once against union leadership, government and employers. In the several years immediately following Allied victory, industrialists sought to recoup concessions made to workers since the late 1930s, while newer members of the industrial workforce (removed southerners, especially blacks, and women retaining their jobs) along with

---

10   Published material on the Johnson-Forest Tendency remains scarce. See James and Grace Lee Boggs, "A Critical Reminiscence," in *Urgent Tasks* 12, also reminiscences of Grace Lee and James Boggs, Nettie Kravitz, Martin Glaberman, Marjorie O'Brien, Leah Dillon Grant, Stan Weir, Steve Zeluck and Raya Dunayevskaya in the Oral History of the American Left Collection, NYU. For microfilmed documents from the Johnson-Forest Tendency, see the Raya Dunayevskaya Papers, Wayne State University.

the returned GIs demanded a piece of the better world they had been promised for past sacrifices. City general strikes and industry-wide actions crossed jurisdictional lines and inspired a blue-collar camaraderie unknown since the sit-down days—but this time frequently critical of unions themselves. Small business and no few labor leaders responded with panic. The Republican Congress and the Truman administration seized the opportunity afforded by the Cold War to blame the unrest (altogether undeservedly) on the Communists and to enact new measures, most notably the Taft-Hartley Act, limiting labor activism. Militant labor suffered a defeat whose sorry consequences remain to this day. But even the pulsating frustration, disappointment and unrealized aspirations fed a creative outburst of popular music, sports and film. The nation seemed to pause between the utopian anti-Nazi zeal slipping away and the social stasis, urban flight and consumer craving of the 1950s.[11]

Such counter-institutional militancy, and the absence of a Socialist or Communist party on a European scale, gave James' political innovations a special urgency. Time was running out. The paucity of actual Trotskyists, however, may in retrospect raise questions about James' contemporary optimism. I once frankly asked him how he thought a movement of several hundred could expect to change a country of a hundred million. Behind the famous Marxist confidence in historical logic, behind the infamous Trotskyist grouplet striving for the correct political position, might be found an intellectual's resolve. His many intellectual friends of the time shared James' political conclusions domestic and international but felt helpless, isolated, impotent. The atomic annihilation of Hiroshima and Nagasaki, the full reports of the Holocaust, deepened the sense of paralysis. The cultivated Jewish sensitivity which balanced proletarian-revolutionary commitment with love for Toscanini and fascination with psychoanalysis had been the Shachtman group's existential *raison d'être*. Now, as the promised political breakthrough for the group failed to appear, and so much of the world situation appeared bleak, the collective will gave way. Years before the group shriveled in size and its foremost leaders turned sharply to the right, pessimism suffused the cadres.

---

11   The best account of this era is in George Lipsitz, *Class and Culture in Cold War America: "A Rainbow at Midnight"* (New York: Bergin/Praeger, 1982).

James' circle had an almost unique sense of actual optimism within or outside the Shachtman group. Unlike Communists or liberals, the "Johnson-Forest Tendency" based its hopes not on Allied victory and post-war Russo-American cooperation in a state-regulated world order, but rather in the instinctive rebellion against that order. Unlike the Shachtmanites (or their opposing twin, the Socialist Workers Party led by James P. Cannon), they believed the possibilities of mass mobilization had drastically altered the revolutionaries' own role.

The group first proposed to convert the rest of the Troskyists to its evolving position. James insisted the Workers' Party "recognize its function as a group making propaganda for revolutionary action to the masses," i.e., leap over the anticipated party-building stage almost entirely. When other leaders pointed to the political and cultural "backwardness" of American labor as proof of the need for an educational-organizational interregnum before the decisive battle with capitalism, James brought forward his own prognostications. Lenin, James argued, had late in life repudiated the instrumental elitism of *What Is to Be Done?*, the dogma that only the revolutionary could educate workers. The great Bolshevik leader saw correctly that the strategic position of Russian workers in the economy and urban society thrust them into a pivotal role regardless of other factors. Moreover, James added, the American proletariat had other special sources of strength. The social-democratic reformism dominant in Western Europe, the European Communist Parties' restraint on workers, had no strength here. As so frequently in our brutal industrial history, American class forces faced off against each other virtually unmediated. "The American proletariat," James concluded, "is literally revolting against the very conditions of production itself."[12]

Among a series of documents outlining the "Johnson-Forest Tendency" perspectives, *The Invading Socialist Society*, published in 1947 just as the group prepared entry into the Socialist Workers Party, provides the decisive break with the older positions and foreshadows *State Capitalism and World Revolution*. Here, James argued for the first time that

---

12   *Balance Sheet: Trotskyism in the United States, 1940–47, The Workers Party and the Johnson-Forest Tendency* (Johnson-Forest Tendency, 1947), 11. This document traces the internal evolution of the group better than any other. *The Balance Sheet Completed*, a lesser document published three years later, concludes the odyssey through American Trotskyism.

Communist parties were not essentially "tools of the Kremlin" as Trotskyist orthodoxists claimed, but rather "an organic product of the mode of capitalism at this stage." Seen in that way, a new objective layer of intelligentsia and union leadership disillusioned with private capitalism but unable to see workers' capacity for self-rule could be understood as a result of historical dialectics. Stalinism ceased to be viewed as a grotesque and ultimately inexplicable distortion of the revolutionary process. To the contrary, it had to be a "necessary and inevitable form of development of the labor movement." James refused to be drawn into the blanket anti-communism which singled out Russia as the main enemy to progress and its American supporters as the main opponents that Trotskyists had to overcome. He perceived the similarity in Communist and Trotskyist supporters of various bureaucratic tendencies, and he drew a strategic conclusion: "It is the task of the Fourth International to drive as clear a line between bourgeois nationalization and proletarian nationalization as the revolutionary Third International drove between bourgeois democracy and proletarian democracy."[13] James had only to detach the goal from the Trotskyist means.

State Capitalism and World Revolution may itself be regarded as a step toward the philosophical conclusion spelled out in Facing Reality, written with Grace Lee and published in 1958 when James had already gone into exile. There, James took positive cognizance of the American black movement, the nationalist revolutions in Asia and Africa, and above all the Hungarian Revolution of 1956. These had begun to carry out, albeit in different ways, the hopes expressed in his Trotskyist years. He also drew moral conclusions that the strictures of Trotskyism had not allowed. He judged the arms race, the stifling official culture and the ethical bankruptcy of East and West alike as decisive proof that "Official society is not in decline. As civilization, as culture, as reason, as morals, it is already dead."[14] The reader can judge,

---

13   C.L.R. James, F. Forest, and Ria Stone (i.e., Raya Dunayevskaya and Grace Lee), *The Invading Socialist Society*, 1972 edition (Bewick Editions) of the 1947 original publication. Reprinted in *A New Notion: Two Works by C.L.R. James* (Oakland: PM Press, 2010).
14   *Facing Reality*, by C.L.R. James, Grace Lee, and Pierre Chaulieu (i.e., Paul Cardan, pseudonym of Cornelius Castoriadis of the *Socialisme ou Barbarie* group in France; Chaulieu reportedly did not really collaborate on this book, but added his authorship for strategic reasons), *Facing Reality*, 1974 edition (Detroit: Bewick Editions) of the 1958 original publication, 44. See Paul Berman's penetrating comments on this "underground classic" in "Facing Reality" in *Urgent Tasks* 12 and *C.L.R. James: His Life and Work*.

in the following text, how far James had already gone along the road to this larger view in 1950. *State Capitalism and World Revolution* is also the last of James' texts to be set in the classic Marxist-Leninist strategic framework. *Facing Reality* seemed to many a *de facto* anarchism, the authors' disclaimers notwithstanding. Sheared away from the last of the vanguard moorings, the revolutionary group had lost its cadre-building mission between the waves of radical upsurge; its political role became uncertain. Here, in a concrete political sense, James' group foreshadowed the successes and limitations of the New Left. It could publish a newspaper remarkably lively and optimistic for its day (the early 1950s), seize upon the implications of phenomena (wildcat strikes or the first stirrings of Black Power in the unions) better than the doctrine-ridden Left, and encourage young people with its wide-ranging belief in human creativity. It could not so easily maintain, or even justify its own separate existence. James himself was wont to say that the group through its various emanations, from its official abandonment of Trotskyism in 1950 to its formal dissolution in 1970, knew what it was moving away from but not so clearly what it was going toward. James had completed a philosophical journey, had seen more clearly than any other political thinker of the older generation the fresh phase of organization and attitude up ahead—but at a cost.[15] *State Capitalism and World Revolution* told the Old Left what it did not want to hear, and spoke to the rising New Left in a voice that it could not clearly understand.

Now, in the 1980s, circumstances have once again shifted, and this time favorably for the forgotten text. More massively, more completely than the 1956 Hungarian Revolution or the 1968 French revolt, Polish Solidarity has truly vindicated James. Concurrently, the most drastic reduction of workers' living standards since the late nineteenth century has brought class issues (if not their solution) home to Europeans and Americans. We live in a world where the revolutionary chiliasm of bleeding Latin America and the collapse of labor officialdom at the imperial centers have become inextricably intertwined, the distance between the

---

15   Accounts of the later James group activities are still more scarce. See the reminiscence of a sympathetic outsider, "Young Detroit Radicals, 1955–1965," by Dan Georgakas, in *Urgent Tasks* 12 and *C.L.R. James: His Life and Work.*

"utopian" wish for total change and the action required by survival now reduced to a thin edge of stubborn reality.[16]

James has had a way of seeing the faces of the crowd behind the glamour and horror of the economic-political spectacle. No wonder social historians as a group have been the quickest to appreciate the significance of his contribution. The meta-theory of *State Capitalism and World Revolution* has been the most difficult aspect of his legacy to apprehend and assimilate, perhaps, because the human basis of all social forces remains most hidden. All the same, the reader will find that the text's inner meaning peeps out above the nearly forty years' distance from its original publication, and above all the difficulties of context and language.

The proof lies in Chapter XI. *State Capitalism and World Revolution* ends, save for two pages, with a universal perception. Treatises have been written by quantum physicists, testaments delivered by Native American seers, warnings proclaimed by poets and natural scientists against the calamity that the mechanist perception of the universe has caused in our environment and in our way of understanding life. We can see far better now than in 1950 how the Western conception of conquering Nature is related to an attitude about the use of human beings as mere functions of production and consumption. Every day we count the toll in mounting cancer cases and the devastation of some natural setting or species of flora or fauna eons in creation. We seem to have reserved a prime spot for ourselves in the list of future extinctions. All of James cried out against this world-view when it still held Marxism firmly in its grip.[17] Behind his dialectical critique—not denial of Marxism's and Bolshevism's limitations but transcendence which retains the best of tradition—thrives a personal insight both unique and universally human, characteristic not only of James but of his whole political circle. Let him tell a story about the origins of that insight, from the pages of his unpublished autobiography:

I remember my first break with the philosophy of rationalism. It was Bergson, 1934. His work had come at the turn

16 See "C.C. Interviews James on Poland," *Cultural Correspondence* 2 (Winter 1983): 20.

17 Paul Buhle and Jim Murray, "West Indies Microcosm—Interview," in *Free Spirits: Annals of the Insurgent Imagination*, Vol. I, edited by Paul Buhle et al. (San Francisco: City Lights Books, 1982), 91–93.

of the century. And was startling to me on two counts. 1) He attacked the abstractions of Understanding, their mechanical categorization, etc., and opposed to this, Intuition. 2) Humor, he said, was the fulfillment of the desire to see the snob and aristocrat humbled. So that the well-dressed man slipping on a banana peel was his classic example of humor. It is still individualistic, as it would be in this philosopher, but I remember it broke me with morbid and melancholy philosophy speculation.[18]

Paul Buhle

---

18   From notes for an unpublished autobiography.

Preface to the Third Edition
(1968)

WHEN THE SECOND edition of *State Capitalism and World Revolution* was at the printer, the Hungarian Revolution exploded. It could only be acknowledged in a few paragraphs on the cover. Now, while this third edition is being prepared, the totality of what was put forward in this document is revealed in the revolutionary struggles of French workers and students. These struggles are not over as this is being written.

In the years since the second edition of *State Capitalism and World Revolution* was published in England much of what was contained in this document has been accepted by a wider public. What was first said here in 1950 became visible to many after the thaw in the Cold War and the increase in travel and communication between the nations of the West and of the East. The characteristics which the Soviet Union shared with all capitalist countries could be seen directly. It no longer had to be culled from statistical analyses or from reading between the lines of speeches to congresses of the Communist Party of the Soviet Union.

Yet this work is not only not out of date, it is more valuable than ever. For its significance has only incidentally been its accurate description of Russian and Western European society. The importance of this book is that it refined and brought up to date the theory of Marxism and made it directly applicable to our own time.

What is most often overlooked by those who accept entirely or in part the conception that the Soviet Union and its related states are fundamentally capitalist is that this analysis is an analysis of capitalist society, not Russian society. The conclusions flowing from this analysis have the greatest relevance in understanding the United States as well as the Soviet Union, Great Britain as well as Poland, France as well as China, and, of course, the working class of all these countries. Capitalism is an international society and the working class is a class that transcends national borders. Marx's description of nineteenth century England did not describe nineteenth century France or Germany. But the conclusions which Marx drew from his study of Great Britain were applicable everywhere.

In Chapter V, The Class Struggle, "The Mode of Labor in the United States" is set down side by side with "The Mode of Labor in Russia." The specific form of class relations in Russia led to Vorkuta, to the German revolt of 1953, to the Polish and Hungarian Revolutions and to the Workers' Councils as the new form of the workers' struggles. But that form is as international as the Commune was in 1871, as Soviets were in 1905 and 1917. Not in detail but in essence—otherwise—all theory is nonsense or theory becomes a universal theory of national exceptionalism.

For the last twelve years the Hungarian Revolution has been evidence of the concrete stage of the struggle for socialism. It had established in life what could only be established in the abstractness of theory before. It began with the total destruction of the vanguard party as any kind of revolutionary instrument. It indicated how far in advance of 1917 the world of the 1950s was. An educated, modern working class did not require indirect methods of representation. In the Workers' Councils it created the instruments of direct democracy, what has been called in the United States, participatory democracy. This, of course, has nothing in common with the "participation" of de Gaulle or the workers' councils of Tito, both of which are designed so that workers can participate in their own exploitation. The Hungarian working class did not require separate instruments to control other sections of society. Farmers, office-workers, technicians, civil servants—all created their own equivalent of workers' councils to manage their own affairs in the name of the revolution as a whole. Instead of workers or students taking over such strategic instruments as radio stations and newspapers, the staffs of these institutions made their own revolution. Only in the totality of the Hungarian Revolution does much of what has been happening in the United States in the years since 1956 become clear. The refusal of the black liberation movement to confine itself to the limits of a single traditional organization; the constant search for, and experimentation with, new social and organizational forms on the part of black militants, students and middle class anti-war fighters; the resistance of American workers to union-imposed contracts and procedures: all are reflections of the new stage that emerged in Hungary in 1956.

Now, in 1968, the struggle is renewed in France. In 1950 the following was noted in *State Capitalism and World Revolution*: "The Stalinist leaders aim to control the mass proletarian mobilization in exactly the same manner as de Gaulle aims to control those of the petty-bourgeoisie. The Leninist party in 1950, in practice where it can, but in theory always, must be the expression of the mass proletarian mobilization aimed against the bureaucracy as such. This bureaucracy in Russia, in France and Italy (even where it is in opposition) and in the United States is the embodiment of the Plan of state-capitalism" (57). The revolution in France has already carried the theory of 1950 and the events of 1956 further. It is necessary to say now that Communist Party, Social Democratic Party, Trade Unions, all are bourgeois institutions. They can neither speak for nor negotiate for the revolution. The revolution is not the means by which workers achieve new, socialist institutions to replace the old, bourgeois institutions. The revolution is the means by which the socialist institutions emerge and destroy the bourgeois institutions which restrain them.

The mode of labor in the United States, that is, the specific form of relations between the working class and its oppressors, also reflects this new stage and must lead to an American equivalent of workers' councils. "The bureaucracy inevitably must substitute the struggle over consumption, higher wages, pensions, education, etc. for a struggle in production. This is the basis of the welfare state, the attempt to appease the workers with the fruits of labor when they seek satisfaction in the work itself. The bureaucracy must raise a new social programme in the realm of consumption because it cannot attack capitalism at the point of production without destroying capitalism itself" (41). Since that was written it has been demonstrated in many ways. Negatively, the bureaucracy (especially of the former CIO unions) have demonstrated that they are no longer the simple, corrupt agents of capitalists as were their old-line AFL antecedents. John L. Lewis of the miners, Walter Reuther of the auto workers, Harry Bridges of the longshoremen, and their brothers in other industrial unions have long demonstrated their willingness to participate directly in the management of production and the disciplining of rank-and-file workers through the union contract and the grievance procedure. No matter how modified the form, this is no longer the traditional behavior of the labor fakers of the epoch of imperialism. This xxviii State Capitalism and World Revolution

is the Stalinism (or, perhaps, neo-Stalinism) of the labor bureaucracy in the epoch of state capitalism. It should be clear that the term, Stalinism, is not being used in the narrow sense of a faction of the Communist Party. The same distinction is needed to understand the difference between Attlee and Wilson, who were and are determined that the Labour Party shall administer British capitalism, and Macdonald and his brethren of pre–World War II, who were equally determined that it should not. These are the bureaucrats (in the United States, in Great Britain and elsewhere) whom the Marxist sectarians are determined to educate to their "responsibilities," or replace with more efficient bureaucrats.

The workers, of course, have other ideas. The massive 1955 wildcats in the UAW for the first time openly counterposed "the struggle in production" to "the struggle over consumption." To Reuther's new national agreement which included the precedent-setting Supplemental Unemployment Benefits, the workers replied with "specific local grievances" which, in their tens of thousands, ran the gamut of life in the factory and indicated the determination of the workers to control production. Since then the process has expanded and intensified, leaving very few industries untouched. In this struggle, Marxist methodology requires that the Hungarian workers' councils act as a goal and a guide. When workers are clearly rejecting the concept of a return to the beginnings of the union, when they are searching for new forms of organization, it is not the function of conscious revolutionists to urge them to confine their struggle to the limits set by labor bureaucrats and the requirements of capitalist production. It is necessary to describe the struggle as it really is—the search by American workers for their equivalent of the workers' councils. The only alternative is to pretend that the trade unions can perform some kind of revolutionary function, something they have never been able to do, even under considerably more favorable circumstances.

The conception that there is a revolutionary potential in the American trade union movement has been rejected by American workers. But this serves still to mislead numbers of radicals looking for ways in which to fight the American imperialist colossus by helping to conceal the fundamental division between workers and union officials and the deadly war that goes on constantly between them. It is only ignorance of this war which can lead to theories that proclaim the incorporation of

the workers into the Establishment (or the disappearance of the working class altogether). It is a peculiar view which believes that workers
who have won themselves, through decades of the bitterest and most
violent class struggle, increased incomes, private homes and cars, refrig-
erators and television sets, are therefore more likely to enter the factory
each morning of their lives and accept without serious argument inhu-
man, totalitarian treatment that is a combination of the penitentiary and
the kindergarten. Quite the contrary: only the struggles, the explosions,
the new forms of organization are inevitable.

The origin of *State Capitalism and World Revolution* as a document that was presented to the Trotskyist movement required that it
have polemical elements although it was the positive presentation of
a profoundly new analysis. This has resulted in its containing names
that would be unfamiliar to the ordinary reader. Pablo and Germain
were the political pseudonyms of European Trotskyists who held differ-
ing views on the problems under discussion. Faced with the collapse of
Trotsky's theory, Pablo represented a new orthodoxy which sacrificed
Marxist methodology in order to extend Trotsky's defense of the Soviet
Union to a principle applicable to all Stalinist societies. Germain, not
willing to go that far, introduced an empirical form of exceptionalism to
permit him to decide for himself which Stalinist societies were workers'
states and which were not. Max Shachtman was at the time the head of
the Workers Party, a split-off from the Trotskyist Socialist Workers Party.
The Workers Party, after a series of metamorphoses, was dissolved into
the Socialist Party, of which Shachtman is part of its extreme right wing.

The origin of this work as the collective viewpoint of the Johnson-
Forest Tendency also dictated that its authorship be anonymous. It is
gratifying to be able to record that, with the kinds of assistance from
other members of his grouping that are usual for political documents,
the author was C.L.R. James. Perhaps this will help to place James, who
wrote for a number of years under the pseudonym of J.R. Johnson, in a
truer light as a major inheritor and continuator of the Marxist tradition.

Martin Glaberman

Author's Preface to the
Second Edition
(1956)

STATE CAPITALISM AND *World Revolution* was originally published in 1950. The origin of the document is as follows.

The only serious theoretical opposition to Stalinism was that provided over the years by Leon Trotsky. But by the end of World War II, it was obvious that Trotsky's theories no longer had any relation to reality. In the United States, the Johnson-Forest Tendency, a minority of the Trotskyist Socialist Workers Party, decided to present to the 1950 Convention of the Party, not a political resolution of the traditional type, but a long overdue restatement of Marxism for our day. The fact that after six crowded years, it can be reprinted exactly as it was written (with the addition of one word, accidentally omitted in the original) is, we believe, sufficient testimony to the soundness of its theoretical premises.

There is only one test of any theory and that is experience, life itself. In April 1956, the Russian jet plane that landed at London Airport announced the existence in Russia of a modern industry and, with it, a modern proletariat. Relations between workers and management in Western Europe and the United States now form a reliable yardstick for the examination of events and pronouncements in Russia.

With this as guide, Khrushchev's report to the 20th Party Congress makes two things clear. The Russian Communist Party and the Russian unions find themselves in increasing isolation from the all-important productive process of Russia's modern industry. Secondly, under the covering shell of totalitarianism, the actual managers of Russian industry face the same problems as are faced by Dick of Standard's in Coventry or Ford in Detroit and are as baffled by them.

Twenty-five years ago in Britain because of lower levels of tooling, greater craft stratification and the reserve army of unemployed, it was still possible to enforce an effective piece-work system. Its destructive consequences for labor and society were multiplied a thousandfold in the forced industrialization of Russia and was the economic basis of the monstrous regime of Stalin.

Those days are over, both in Britain and in Russia. As line production, the conveyor system and highly divided mass production have developed in Britain, piece-work has clashed more and more with the objective requirements for efficiency. The shop stewards, the shop committees that matured in this period, were not merely economic defense organizations of the workers. They were the only possible means of bringing some order to the chaos caused by the attempts of management to maintain individual piece-work in the new mass-production industries. The workers in Britain have gone a long way toward destroying the piece-work system. On any particular line, or in any particular shop, a minimum is fixed, below which no one may have his wages reduced. By reducing the gap between the minimum and the maximum, the power of the rate-fixer is thereby broken and a levelling of wages takes place. Thus wages are no longer governed by individual effort but by the general level of class struggle in the shop or line concerned. The workers' name for this is *action on the job*. Action on the job goes far beyond trade unionism, for it carries in itself a formidable unity among the workers and gives them a control in every phase of production. This control, though constantly contested by management, is never entirely defeated and steadily expands its scope. Today the center of power moves away from the Labour Party and the unions on to the shop floor. It is from this milieu that have erupted the startlingly revolutionary demands of the Standard workers in Coventry in relation to redundancy. These demands have been watered down by the union leadership into compensation and a vague consultation. The original proposals were based on the conception that men and not capital must henceforth be the primary concern of industry. That conviction is deep in the hearts of many millions all over the world, and its objective realization cannot be long delayed.

How much different is the "planned economy" of Russia? Listen to Khrushchev at the 20th Party Congress:

> Considerable over-fulfillment of such deliberately low output quotas creates the illusion that all is well, and tends to

divert workers, foremen, and engineers from effective efforts to raise productivity. The present practice is to make output quotas correspond in effect to a definite wage level, and not to the technical and efficiency levels already achieved.

It cannot be considered normal that the proportion of basic wages in the total earnings of a worker is no more than 40 to 60 and even less in many enterprises. No time should be lost in bringing order into the system of wage-rates in industry, and clearing the way for introduction on a mass scale of technically substantiated output quotas.

Any British worker knows what that means. The planners plan as they please but the Russian workers, by action on the job, according to their strength from factory to factory, make a wreck of the plans, and particularly in the decisive sphere of the planned productivity.

And what is Khrushchev's remedy?

We are faced by the important political and economic task of introducing proper order into the payment of labor. We must consistently apply the principles of giving workers a personal material incentive, bearing in mind that the realization of this principle is a prime condition for the uninterrupted growth of production. Lenin taught us that "every major branch of the national economy should be based on personal incentive." (*Works*, Russian ed., Vol. 33, 47)

In other words, the Russian super-planner, in the face of the essentially cooperative labor process of modern industry, has no remedy except the Stalinist knout.

Khrushchev, Bulganin, and Suslov sing this song in every conceivable key and thereby show that, despite slave camps, N.K.V.D. and draconic labor laws, it is the workers' shop organizations (probably meeting in secret) which today in Russia as in Britain are setting the norms, levelling the wages and breaking the power of the rate-fixers. The situation of the British Labour Party and the union machinery in face of the dynamic demands and activity of the shop steward movement in Coventry illuminates Khrushchev's panic before the isolation of the Communist

Party, of the Russian unions and of the Russian economists and scientists from production, and frantic exhortations to all of them to enter production, to study production, to master production, etc., etc.

Six years ago *State Capitalism and World Revolution* stated that in this contemporary struggle lay the whole future of industry and therefore of society. Control of the national economy offers certain "technical" advantages to those who control. This was known not only to Lenin but to Marx and Engels. But the Russian state plan can deal only with the crudest approximations such as total input of steel and total output of cars. This had its uses in the Stalinist era, but in modern industry the only cost-accounting that has any serious value is the cost-accounting of the workers on the line, of the thousand and one details of production, constantly organized, checked, modified, discarded and reorganized. This is the only rational production and it can be done only by freely associated men. It is totally beyond state planners of any kind, whether with or without parliamentary democracy. For the moment the enormous creative potentialities of production in these shop organizations are dissipated and even reversed by their use as a defense mechanism against an outmoded managerial class and its political adjuncts.

The writers of the document broke with Trotskyism and its fetishism of "nationalization" to concentrate attention on this process in Russia and in the United States. As distinct from all other theories and analyses, these ideas do not isolate the Russian economy and the Russian workers from the rest of the world. They bring all phenomena into one integrated and growing body of theory, shedding new light as new events unfold.

The anti-Stalin campaign of the Russian and other Communist Parties exemplifies another fundamental thesis of the document which is that, plan or no plan, totalitarianism is an unviable form of government, doomed to perish by its own contradictions. But their diatribes against Stalin, Khrushchev, Malenkov and Mikoyan deal with the shadow and not with the substance, with the effect and not the cause. Democracy in Russia and the satellite states will herald its coming by the emergence into the open of these proletarian organizations which all the evidence goes to show are already clandestinely accepted by Russian factory managers. It is these organizations which save modern industrial production from complete chaos and it has been proved that the Nazi Party and the Gestapo were never able to eliminate such formations from German industry.

The political conclusions of this economic analysis can be summed up in its total repudiation of the theory and practice of the Leninist theory of the Vanguard Party for our era. However, for the Minority to have written that clearly in the document would have invited expulsion from those fanatical Vanguard Partyists, the Trotskyists. The reader, therefore, will have to bear this in mind in reading Chapter VI, The Theory of the Party. Even as it is, it is clear enough, but the following will not be unhelpful.

Each of the three great workers' internationals corresponds in form to a particular stage of capitalism. Lenin's theory and practice of the Vanguard Party, the party of the elite, of the leaders, was admirably adapted to the period 1903–1923. Progressively from that time, it has been a millstone round the neck of the modern proletariat in its struggle for socialism. That this form was no creation of Lenin's Machiavellian brain and is rooted in historical circumstances is shown by the fact that today the Labour Parties and unions, despite important historical variations, function in essence as Vanguard Parties, that is to say with a centralized machine which, in the accepted Stalinist fashion, is far more tolerant to its programmatic enemies than it is to dissident minorities.

What type of new organizations do we propose? We do not propose any.

The great organizations of the masses of the people and the workers in the past were not worked out by any theoretical elite or vanguard. They arose from the experience of millions of people and their need to overcome the intolerable pressures which society had imposed upon them for generations.

The great fact of the present organizations is that they suppress and crush what is always required for the building of a new society, the powers and energies of those who have to build it. Never has there been latent in any society such enormous power, capacities and energies as at present exist in the modern working class and the classes nearest to it. But the bigger the traditional organizations grow and the more power they wield, the more they act as a brake upon these creative energies. So rooted are these organizations in the very structure of society that they can be shaken only by an upheaval in the very foundation of society. It is sufficient to say that in historical terms, the new organizations will come as Lilburne's Leveller Party came, as the sections and popular societies of Paris in 1793, as the Commune in 1871 and the Soviets in 1905, with not a single soul having any concrete ideas about them until they appeared in all their power and glory.

But once we have a clear historical perspective we can see outlines of the future in the rising in Eastern Germany in 1953, the great strike in Nantes in 1955, the general strike against Reuther of the UAW at the very moment he was celebrating his victory of the Guaranteed Annual Wage, the incredible ten-year struggle of the British dockers and now, as we write, the Coventry workers, striding on the national stage, taking the breath away from all observers by the daring and originality of their plans for running a modern economy.

All these struggles, varied as they are in scope and significance, have this in common, that they all embody formations and activity which override, bypass or consciously aim at substituting new social forms for the traditional workers' organizations. However high they soar they build upon shop floor organizations and action on the job. Precisely because America lags behind in traditional workers' organizations the mass of the American people are far advanced in their conception of the plant (and the office) as the center of the life of the community. The new social and political forms corresponding to the needs of modern industry and modern society can well erupt first in that most modern of countries still politically enchained in the eighteenth century politics of Whigs and Tories, otherwise known as Democrats and Republicans.

When the document was written six years ago, all this was mere theoretical prognosis. It is printed now with more confidence as a guide to the great events ahead.

It is not the debates on free speech behind the Iron Curtain which will be decisive in the liberation of these oppressed peoples. It is what took place at Poznan. Like the Berlin rising in June 1953, it came directly from the shop organizations of the workers. The ultimate aim in Coventry, Berlin, Detroit and Poznan is not liberal free speech nor higher wages, "compensation" nor "consultation," but the construction of a new society from the bottom up.

Johnson	Christianson	Chaulieu
Brendel	Massen	Hughes

The signers of this preface do not endorse the details of the analysis or of the conclusions of the document but are agreed that Marxism today can find its way only along the path outlined in it.

Authors' Introduction to the First Edition

In 1940 the theory of Trotskyism seemed founded on a rock. Today, August 4, 1950, this is the situation in the world Trotskyist movement.

1. The "irresponsible" RCP [Revolutionary Communist Party] of Great Britain and a powerful and very responsible minority of U.S. Trotskyists claim that the states in Eastern Europe are workers' states. Pablo's latest position is indistinguishable from theirs.[1]

2. A great majority now accept Yugoslavia, hitherto denounced as a capitalist, totalitarian police-state, as a workers' state.

3. The cornerstone of Trotskyist policy for nearly twenty years, that the nationalization of industry alone gave Russia the claim to be a workers' state, is now vigorously denied; though what then makes it a workers' state is impossible to see because the *Transitional Program* says that politically the Stalinist state does not differ from the Fascist state "save in its more unbridled savagery."

4. Those who are opposed to the states in Eastern Europe being considered workers' states denounce the theory as based upon *exceptional circumstances* and say, rightly, that conclusions would have to be drawn for the whole world. When asked to explain how nationalization took place without the proletarian revolution, these bitter opponents of any theory of *exceptional circumstances* do not hesitate to reply that the nationalizations were due to *exceptional circumstances*. But one of their number, Germain, generalizes the theory of *exceptional circumstances*, and declares that the property relations can be overturned without permitting us to conclude that what we have is a workers' state.

---

1 See "Pablo" and "Germain" in the glossary.

5. Pablo declares:
    (a) Stalinist parties can under exceptional circumstances lead a proletarian revolution. This destroys the historical necessity of the Fourth International.
    (b) We must be prepared to have degenerated workers' states for centuries. This means either that some capitalism (actually American capitalism) will last for that time; or that all proletarian revolutions will be betrayed.

To this pro-Stalinist, liquidationist tendency, now months old, there is no resistance. Under the impact of the events of 1940–50 the theory of the Fourth International is in chaos.

Concretely the Majority and the Minority are now engaged in an unrestrained attempt to establish the closest possible alliance with the Communist Party of Yugoslavia (CPY). To this "Johnson-Forest" are opposed and attribute the action to the prevalence in the International, implicit and explicit, of the ideas expressed by Pablo.

The "Johnson-Forest" Tendency

All tendencies inside world Trotskyism, sharp as the differences may be, have been united in adherence to the fundamental theory of the permanent revolution; in maintaining the traditions of Bolshevism; in irreconcilable opposition to all other tendencies in the labor movement. The ideas put forward by "Johnson-Forest" originate in that common heritage and have no other purpose than to bind us together in the achievement of our aims.

"Johnson-Forest" have abstained almost totally from the Yugoslav discussion and now enter it only to the degree that it is a part of the preparation for definitive decisions.

We ask that our views, however far-reaching, be considered on their merits. We believe that we have earned the right to such a hearing, and more so because in the death-agony of capitalism, the chief spokesman of the Fourth International has called into question the validity of Marxism for our epoch.

We have to mention this because all positions, even Pablo's, claim, and no doubt sincerely, to be interpreting and bringing up to date the basic ideas of Trotsky. We are not doing that. Our position is that the chaos in the International is due to the fact that Trotsky's method of analysis and system of ideas are wrong, and that the chaos in the International will continue to grow until a new system is substituted for the present one.

We are very conscious of the fact that for this system of ideas which we claim must be discarded, thousands have died, and that by it many now living have shaped their lives. But the class position of the proletariat is involved the moment you reach the question of defensism or defeatism. As long as this was confined to Russia, there was no urgent necessity to draw what was implicit to its conclusions. But today the question involves half of Europe and half of Asia, that is to say, the whole world.

I
What Is Stalinism?

Trotsky's Analysis

The first, the basic, the indispensable task of a revolutionary international is to define correctly the working class organization it proposes to overthrow. In this task the failure of orthodox Trotskyism is complete.

The *Transitional Program* asserts: "The definite passing over of the Comintern to the side of the bourgeois order."

Later the same document says: "The Third International has taken to the road of reformism . . . The Comintern's policy . . . demonstrates that the Comintern is likewise incapable of learning anything further or of changing."

In the December 1938 issue of the *New International* we read why: "Ten years ago it was predicted that the theory of socialism in one country must inevitably lead to the growth of nationalist tendencies in the sections of the Comintern. This prediction has become an obvious fact. . . . Today we can predict with assurance the inception of a new stage. The growth of imperialist antagonisms, the obvious proximity of the war danger and the equally obvious isolation of the USSR must unavoidably strengthen the *centrifugal nationalist tendencies* within the Comintern. Each one of its sections will begin to evolve a patriotic policy on its own account. Stalin has reconciled the communist parties of imperialist democracies with their national bourgeoisies." (Emphasis in original).

In the last pages of *The Draft Program of the Comintern* can be seen the prediction that Stalin's theory of socialism in one country would lead the Comintern to disintegration into national sections, like the Social-Democracy on August 4th, 1914.

This is the theory from 1929 to 1938, absolutely clear and absolutely wrong.

It is precisely this question, this and no other which, since the end of World War II, has crippled the French party. To this day the International does not know whether the Chinese Stalinists are enemies of the Chinese bourgeoisie or collaborators with it.

At the World Congress in 1948 those in Europe who held our views moved that the quoted sections be deleted from the *Transitional Program*. The motion was voted down.

Trotsky, basing himself on the experience of 1914–1918, believed that there were two fundamental political currents in the world working class movement. One was reformism, the Second International, based upon private property, the defense of the national state, enemy of the proletarian revolution. The other was revolutionary, based upon or fighting for state-property, repudiating the national state, advocate and defender of the proletarian revolution. Between them were various brands of centrism.

Upon these premises he saw the bureaucracy in Russia as centrist, and inevitably headed, as all bureaucracies, for the restoration of private property. That is why the *Transitional Program* says:

> The fascist, counter-revolutionary elements, *growing un-interruptedly express with ever greater consistency*, the interests of world imperialism. These candidates for the *role of compradors* consider, not without reason, that the new ruling layer can insure their positions of privilege *only* through rejection of nationalization, collectivization and monopoly of foreign trade *in the name of* the assimilation of "Western civilization," i.e., *capitalism*. Between these two poles, there are intermediate, diffused Menshevik-SR-liberal *tendencies which gravitate toward bourgeois democracy*. (48, emphasis added)

And a little later: "From them, i.e., from the right, we can expect ever more determined attempts in the next period to revise the socialist character of the USSR and bring it closer in pattern to 'Western civilization' in its fascist form" (49–50).

Again at the World Congress it was moved to delete this from the *Program*. This was voted down.

Two years after the World Congress, Pablo has come to a decision. When he says that we have to make up our minds to deal with degenerated workers' states for centuries, he is saying that the bureaucracies in Eastern Europe are organically attached to the state-property forms, that they perform a function in production, and this is a form of economy superior to capitalism. The same applies to the Russian bureaucracy, parent and sponsor of the satellite bureaucracies. This, we have to admit, is Trotskyism, logical and complete. Pablo leaves out only the one thing that Trotsky did not leave out, namely, that if this were so, then Marxism is Utopia.

The Analysis of "Johnson-Forest"

"Johnson-Forest" repudiate all this, theory, practice and methodology. We base our analysis on the theory of state-capitalism. It is commonly believed that this has mainly to do with defeatism or defensism of Russia. That is the least of our concerns.

This is the position of "Johnson-Forest":

(a) As the Social-Democrats were the labor bureaucracy of monopoly capitalism, the Stalinists are the labor bureaucracy of the period of "vast state-capitalist trusts and syndicates."

(b) The Stalinists are not class-collaborationists, fools, cowards, idiots, men with "supple spines," but conscious clear-sighted aspirants for world-power. They are deadly enemies of private property capitalism. They aim to seize the power and take the place of the bourgeoisie. When they support a war or do not support, support the bourgeoisie or do not support, they know exactly what they are doing. The bourgeoisie also knows. In fact everybody, including most workers, knows this, except orthodox Trotskyism.

(c) But the Stalinists are not proletarian revolutionists. They aim to get power by help, direct or indirect, of the Red Army and the protection of Russia and the Russian state. That is the reason why they follow the foreign policy of the Kremlin—it is sheer naked self-interest.

(d) Theirs is a last desperate attempt under the guise of "socialism" and "planned economy" to reorganize the means of production without releasing the proletariat from wage-slavery. Historical viability they have none; for state-ownership multiplies every contradiction of capitalism. Antagonisms of an intensity and scope so far unknown already have Stalinism in their grip. Power merely brings these into the open.

(e) The dilemma of the Fourth International is that it has to recognize that there now exists a labor bureaucracy which is the enemy of private property and national defense and yet is counter-revolutionary. The Fourth International cannot escape this decision: if the destruction of private property and the repudiation of national defense are revolutionary, then Stalinism is revolutionary and there is no historical need for a Fourth International.

(f) These are the questions with which the theory of state-capitalism deals. The theory is not primarily concerned with defensism or defeatism in Russia, about which we can do little. We are primarily concerned here with what the refusal to accept this theory does to the party, its solidarity, its capacity to fight its enemies, its capacity to preserve itself and to grow, in brief, to prepare the liquidation of Stalinism.

II
The Stalinists and the Theory of State Capitalism

It is very easy to quote from *In Defense of Marxism* how the Mensheviks stuck to the concrete while Lenin began with dialectical materialism. To carry out Leninism in practice, however, is another matter. Strictly speaking, we should begin with philosophy, but we postpone that to the end of this document where it sums up the whole. We shall begin instead with political economy.

It is not because of the policy of the Fourth International that the world revolution has suffered such defeats. Stalinism is the enemy. We have to pose the question in opposition to Stalinism.

For many years now the whole gigantic theoretical machinery of Stalinism has had one main theoretical enemy. This enemy, it will surprise most members of the Fourth International to learn, is the theory of state-capitalism, whether applied to Russia or countries abroad. We have to add that the Fourth International either does not know or does not care about what the Stalinists are doing in this field. As we shall see, that is not at all accidental but it makes our task particularly difficult. Before we discuss, we have to state the facts and conditions of discussion.

Marx removed political economy from intellectual theorizing and made it a weapon of the class struggle. He placed it in the very heart of the capitalist system, in the process of production itself. For him the fundamental antagonism of society was the contradiction between the development of the productive forces and the social relations of production. Inasmuch as this conception is what the Stalinists are using all the power of the Russian state to destroy, we must spend some time here.

In the United States, since 1935, the working class in the CIO is mobilized to fight *any* increase in the productivity of labor. Speed-up does not mean necessarily work beyond physical or mental endurance. The proletariat as a class is opposed to increase of productivity of labor in any form, whether it is speed-up of the line or the machine, or the further division of labor. It is convinced in the very marrow of its being that any such increase is obtained only at the expense of its own most vital material and spiritual interests. But the capitalist class is equally convinced that the desire of the workers to have the decisive word on production standards is opposed to the vital interests of the capitalist system which they represent. Both sides are absolutely correct upon the basis of capitalist production. The clash is final and absolute.

Marx established that as long as the proletariat did not rule production, production knew and could know no other method of progress but the increase of constant capital, machinery, mechanization, at the expense of variable, living labor. The *only* revolution which could save society was the proletarian revolution in the process of production.

Further he showed that this system not only created the violent clash in social relations. Inevitably the rate of profit would fall and (theoretically) at a certain stage the economy would not be able to expand any further because it would lack sufficient surplus value.

In his strictly logical theory Marx expressly excluded any idea that the system would collapse because goods could not be sold. In his analysis of collapse he made it absolutely clear that the capitalist could sell all the goods he produced. This would not alter the conditions of the workers in the factory. It is possible to keep silent about this, but to deny it—that is impossible. The Stalinists do not go so far. All Marx's theories of crisis, overproduction, commercial crisis, etc., to which he paid careful attention, all are based on this foundation of relations in production.

All his opponents, however differentiated among themselves, are united in this, that they see the solution of the crisis of capitalism in every conceivable place except the reorganization of the productive process by labor itself. From Section 1, Chapter 1, Vol. 1 of *Capital*, this is precisely what Marx opposed. The very categories he used, and the content he gave to them as categories of exploitation, were derived from his analysis of the mode of labor, and without it he could not have succeeded in defeating all his opponents.

It is obvious, therefore, that the Marxian theory from its very elements is an invincible weapon against the capitalist class or a usurping bureaucracy, whether the property is private property or state-property. It is equally obvious that a bureaucracy, caught in the throes of economic crisis and in the name of Marxism exploiting millions of workers, has a deadly enemy in this theory. If the Marxian categories apply to Russia, then it is a simple matter to say that Russia is a form of state-capitalism. The Marxist categories therefore become for the Stalinist bureaucracy the concrete theoretical enemy.

The Stalinists Revise Marx's *Capital*

In 1943 Leontiev published his celebrated *Political Economy in the Soviet Union*. There was a crisis in political economy in the Soviet Union. He tells us that for years *the teaching of political economy had stopped entirely*. The reason will astonish most of the readers of this document. The Soviet youth studying *Capital* found themselves unable to see how the categories, money, wages, etc., as described in *Capital* differed from the categories as they appeared in the Russian reality. (No such doubts trouble orthodox Trotskyists.) Leontiev described the measures adopted. Economists were henceforth to teach:

   (a) that these categories existed before capitalism, hence are not integral to capitalism;
   (b) that they meant something different in each period and hence mean something different in Russia.

Thus Marx's analysis of the categories of capitalism, the foundation of Marxism, received the first blow. But the Stalinist theoreticians had something positive to substitute.

Above all, they said, these categories have always been part and parcel of private property capitalism and exploitation of man by man. There is no private property in Russia, hence no exploitation of man by man, hence these categories are not the same.

But this ridiculous sophistry could not shake *Capital*.

Two years later the Stalinists had to drop the pretense that only the "teaching" of political economy was being changed. Nothing short of a break with the dialectic structure of *Capital* would do. They decided to reorganize *Capital* thoroughly, beginning with page 1 of Chapter 1 of Volume 1. Marx had begun the analysis of capitalism with the analysis of the commodity. The Stalinists repudiated his method, stating that to "preserve unchanged the same sequence" would be "ludicrous and harmful pedantry." The new theory was explained for English readers in *Marx's Capital: An Aid to the Study of Political Economy* by Leontiev, 1946. The Stalinists have drowned Marx's specific categories of capitalist exploitation. They have to, because they cannot differentiate them from the economic system in Russia. They know who the enemy is. In his article Leontiev thundered against the "Trotskyite-Bukharinist wreckers":

> It is known that enemies of socialism of various brands— bourgeois economist wreckers, restorers of capitalism from the camp of the Trotskyite-Bukharinist agency of fascism—have tried to extend to socialist economy the laws of capitalist economy. To suit their wrecking counter- revolutionary purposes they have slanderously perverted the character of the socialist relations that have been introduced among us, falsifying them, repainting them in the colors of capitalist relations.

We hope no one believes that the Stalinists go through all this merely for "Trotskyite-Bukharinist-fascists." To anyone who knows them and reads Leontiev's article, it is perfectly obvious that there is inside Russia itself a tendency to call Russia state-capitalism and the Stalinists can only fight it by mutilating *Capital*. They must attempt in theory as well as in practice to destroy every manifestation of the developing revolution in Russia. The theory of state-capitalism is the theoretical foundation for this revolution.

The Stalinists and the Falling Rate of Profit

Orthodox Trotskyism lives peaceably while all this goes on. It repeats: State-property, therefore no laws of capitalism. The whole meaning of the present discussion is that those days are over.

But what about overproduction, asks orthodox Trotskyism? There can be no overproduction in Russia, hence the system is superior, etc., etc. The Stalinists are taking care of that too. The method is to destroy the theory of the falling rate of profit and substitute the theory of the market, under-consumptionism. *If* state-property, and not the total

reorganization of labor, is the solution to the contradiction of capitalism, then the proletariat has only to work hard (and very hard) until in
the fullness of time, there is enough for all.

In 1943, Leontiev wrote in his essay a moderate paragraph which
looked innocent but was part of the assault on *Capital* and the Russian
proletariat: ". . . the law of value under capitalism operates through the
law of the average rate of profit, whereas in the socialist system of national economy the law of the average rate of profit has lost its significance."

Thus, in place *of the law in the decline in the rate of profit*, i.e., the
insoluble contradiction of capitalism due to value production, the
Stalinists have substituted the average rate of profit or the *distribution*
of the total profits among the capitalists. The average rate of profit is
singled out as the crucial feature of Volume III of *Capital*.[1]

Prior to World War I, the debates in the Marxist movement revolved
around Volume II of *Capital*. The theory of accumulation was urgent
only insofar as it concerned whether imperialist expansion could solve
the contradictions of capitalism. By World War II this was no longer the
question. Not only had the contradictions of capitalism not been solved
by imperialist expansion; there was a crisis in productivity on a world
scale. The debate of necessity has shifted from Volume II (expanded re-
production) to Volume III (decline in the rate of profit).

The debate over Volume III of *Capital* is the debate over the developing revolution on a world scale and especially in Russia. If the problem is selling goods, then there is absolutely no economic reason for the
collapse of the bureaucracy. If, however, the problem is the rate of surplus value in production, needed for expansion, then the bureaucracy is
faced with a revolution in the process of production itself.

It will be possible to fill twenty volumes of books with quotations
about overproduction from Marx and Marxists. *In this dispute* they will
have the same validity as the numerous witnesses the chicken-stealer
was prepared to bring who *hadn't* seen him steal the chickens. They

---

1 Insignificant minority as were "Johnson-Forest," we did what we could to defend Marxist theory against the Stalinist revision. Through the agency of Raya
Dunayevskaya, we forced publication of the document by translating it, attacked
Leontiev and routed the chief Stalinist fellow-travellers in the United States who
came to his defense (*American Economic Review*, September 1944–September 1945,
inclusive).

will not alter the fact that Marx's theory of capitalist collapse is based (though not exclusively) upon the falling rate of profit. It assumes that all the goods are sold, there is no overproduction, and yet capitalism will collapse. The importance of this for the analysis of Stalinist Russia is obvious. It destroys the Stalinist contention that because Russia, unlike capitalism, has no problem of sale of goods, the Russian economy is superior.

We have in many places taken up this question in full. Here we can only state the case:

As late as 1935, Maurice Dobb, British Stalinist, says,

> consumption was an incident—an important incident—in the total setting.... At the same time it remained *only* a facet; and it seems clear that Marx considered the contradiction within the sphere of production—the contradiction between growing productive power, consequent on accumulation, and falling profitability of capital, between the productive forces and the productive relations of capitalist society—as the essence of the matter. (*Political Economy and Capitalism*, 121)

No kind of underconsumptionism could pass as Marxism chiefly because Lenin (who wrote constantly of anarchy of production, individual appropriation, etc.) had nevertheless written the finest analysis of *Capital* in existence, a devastating and comprehensive polemic against all who tried to say that capitalism would collapse because it could not "*realize*" profit, i.e., sell its goods.[2]

Eugene Varga in Russia, however (with some sneaking apologetics, for Varga knows better), for years propagated the view that capitalism would collapse from underconsumption while the nationalized production could not. Then in 1942 appeared *The Theory of Capitalist Development* by Paul Sweezy. Sweezy posed two fundamental types of crises: "In the one case we have to do with movements in the rate of

---

2 See especially the first chapter of his *Capitalism in Russia*, "Theoretic Mistakes of the Nafodnik-Economists," translated into English by F. Forest, *New International* (October, November, December, 1943).

surplus value and the composition of capital, with the value system remaining intact."

This is the Marxist view, the political economy of the proletariat. Paul Sweezy has another view. He goes on to say: "In the other case we have to do with as yet unspecified forces tending to create a general shortage in effective demand for commodities" (146).

This is the political economy of underconsumption. Previously it could be used to some degree by the petty-bourgeoisie. Today it is the absolutely inescapable political economy of the bureaucracy.

Marx's analysis showed that inevitably, though the mass of profit would grow, *total* profit in relation to total capital would grow less and less, and theoretically, would bring the system to a standstill. It is only after having proved this that Marx takes up overproduction, etc.[3]

Sweezy says that Marx's analysis of the falling rate of profit seems to be some rough notes he just jotted down.[4] He scoured the three volumes of *Capital* in an attempt to prove his underconsumptionist interpretation. He could find nothing but some odd scraps which were already notorious as completely inadequate. He had to admit as much (178).

But Sweezy would not give up. Instead he proposes: "Another view is possible, however, namely, that in these scattered passages Marx was giving advance notice of a line of reasoning which, if he had lived to complete his theoretical work, would have been of primary importance in the overall picture of the capitalist economy."

---

3   The falling rate of profit is no longer theory. Like so much of Marx's abstract analysis the proof now is before our eyes. Who in his senses today thinks that the world is suffering from an excess of capital? Where? In Britain, in France, in Italy, in Japan, in India, in Brazil, in China? Where, pray, where? From everywhere the cry rises for capital. The total mass of surplus value produced in relation to the total social capital is hopelessly inadequate. It may be useful (though we doubt this) to point out the fabulous profits of this or that company in the United States. This is no more than a variety of American exceptionalism. These profits will never be able to rebuild world economy. Europe, China, India under capitalism will perish for lack of capital to continue ever-greater expansion. This capitalist system is finished, finished for good and all. Only the released proletariat can produce sufficient to rebuild society. No one has to read Marxism any longer to understand this. All that is necessary is to look.

4   Comrades should not spend all their indignation on this. They will need some a few pages later and not for Sweezy.

So that in thirty years and nearly 3,000 pages Marx was merely giving advance notice.

Sweezy's book was written in 1942. Since then, in the latest issue of *Science and Society* (Spring 1950), this fellow-traveller has become the authentic voice of the Stalinist maneuver to defend Russia against the theory of state-capitalism. As usual, the maneuver takes the form of historical analysis. As always, it seeks desperately to remove the class struggle from the process of production. In this article, Sweezy has reached the advanced stage of replacing the Marxist concept of the internal contradiction in production with a wholly external contradiction, between production for use and production for the market.

We hope, therefore, that this ghost of overproduction which has stalked about in our movement so long and disrupted economic analysis of Russia will go to its grave and stay there; or if it reappears will be injected by its sponsors, however temporarily, with some real blood and life.

III
Lenin and State Capitalism

EQUALLY INSTRUCTIVE IS the Stalinist treatment of state-capitalism and planning. Here a little history is necessary.

It was Marx in *Capital* (Vol. 1, Kerr edition, 688), who stated that the only limit to centralization was all the capital in a single country in the hands of a single corporation. If this is not the economic form of state-capitalism, what is it? It was not a chance remark. He did not have it in the first edition. He wrote it into the second edition with some other points and asked all to note that the additions possessed "a scientific value independent of the original." On this no word, not a word from the Stalinists, and not a word from orthodox Trotskyism.

In *Anti-Dühring* Engels writes the passages so well known that we shall not quote them. They are so clear that there were members of the Workers' Party who discussed them with the cynicism that Engels was a "Johnsonite." It was either this or saying that "Johnson-Forest" were followers of Engels. They preferred the first. Marx, it is known, approved Engels' draft.

In his criticism of the Erfurt Program, Engels attacked the formulation that there was no plan in capitalism. He ends: "And if we pass from joint companies to trusts which command and monopolize entire branches of industry, then we not only cease to have private production but we cease to have planlessness."

Karl Kautsky, while denying that capitalism can plan, never thought of denying statification. In 1907 Kautsky wrote in explanation of the Erfurt Program: "The final result must be the concentration of all the instruments of production in the hands of one person or one stock company, to be used as private property and be disposed of at will; the whole machinery of production will be turned into a gigantic concern subject to a single master" (*The Class Struggle: The Erfurt Program*, Kerr, 1910).

13

Lenin's treatment of the whole question is a model of Marxism. In *Imperialism* (1915), he writes only of monopoly capitalism. Then you can trace how stage by stage he reaches state-monopoly capitalism in the preface to *State and Revolution* (1917).

In the Spring of 1917, in his first report in Russia on the Political Situation, Lenin described how during the war capitalism had developed even more than before the war. Then: "As early as in 1891, i.e., twenty-seven years ago . . . Engels maintained that capitalism could not be regarded any longer as being planless. This idea has become obsolete; once there are trusts, planlessness disappears. . . . Monopoly in general has evolved into state-monopoly" (*Collected Works, Revolution of 1917, Book I,* 282).

Then comes a paragraph in which he separates himself from the whole underlying political economy of the Fourth International: "General conditions show that the war has accelerated the development of capitalism; it advanced from capitalism to imperialism; from monopoly to nationalization. All this made the socialist revolution closer and created the objective conditions for it. Thus the course of the war has brought the socialist revolution nearer to us."

Although Kautsky, for example, had a different theory from Lenin on state-capitalism, all Marxists (until the Fourth International) agreed on this, that the centralization of capital, however great, did not lessen but increased the crisis of capitalism. It is in the theory of the degenerated workers' state that our whole movement has learned to see in a completely centralized capital, regeneration, progress for capitalism.

In the reply to the debate, Lenin quoted from the resolution on which he was speaking: "Monopoly capitalism is changing into state-monopoly capitalism. Social regulation of production and distribution is, under the pressure of circumstances, being introduced in many countries" (316).

He says again:

It is noteworthy that twenty-seven years ago Engels pointed out that to characterize capitalism as something distinguished by its planlessness, means to overlook the role played by trusts, and is unsatisfactory. . . . This remark of Engels is particularly appropriate now, when we have state-monopoly capitalism. The introduction of planning into industry keeps the workers enslaved none the less, though it enables the capitalists to gather in their profits in a more planful way. We now witness the metamorphosis of capitalism into a higher, a regulated form of capitalism.

And here must be noted a remarkable thing. Obviously that resolution on which Lenin was speaking would be a very important document. The Stalinist archivists say that no copy can be found. Be that as it may, as we have shown in *The Invading Socialist Society* (5 onward), the whole, yes, the whole strategy of the October Revolution was built on this.

In *State and Revolution*, Lenin says that the trusts cannot, of course, plan production completely but however much they do plan, they cannot avoid the contradictions of capitalism.

Not mere nationalization, even "confiscation," Lenin repeated and repeated, means military penal labor for the workers; you must have workers' control of production under a Soviet state. The theoreticians of Stalinism avoid all this like the plague.

Then in 1918 Lenin throws his whole weight against the Left-Communists, basing himself upon this theory:

> To elucidate the question still more, let us first of all take the most concrete example of state capitalism. Everybody knows what this example is. It is Germany. Here we have "the last word" in modern large-scale capitalist technique and planned organization, subordinated to *Junker-bourgeois imperialism*. Cross out the word in italics, and in place of the militarist, *Junker*-bourgeois imperialist *state*, put a *state*, but of a different social type, of a different class content—a *Soviet*, that is, a proletarian state, and you will have the *sum-total* of the conditions necessary for socialism. (*Selected Works* VII, 364–65)

He says again: "At present, petty-bourgeois capitalism prevails in Russia, and it is *one and the same road* that leads from it to large-scale capitalism *and* to socialism, through *one and the same* intermediary station called 'national accounting and control of production and distribution.' Those who fail to understand this are committing an unpardonable mistake in economics" (Ibid., 366).

And once again he refers to his previous work on the question of state-capitalism: "In order to convince the reader that this is not the first time I have given this 'high' appreciation of state capitalism and that I gave it before the Bolsheviks seized power I take the liberty of quoting the following passage from my pamphlet *The Threatening Catastrophe and How to Fight It* written in September, 1917" (Ibid., 367).

When he introduced the NEP [New Economic Policy], Lenin quoted this passage to the extent of three pages. Lenin did not know German Fascism or the United States economy during the war, but his whole method shows that in his usual manner, always watching the stages, he would have had not the slightest difficulty with Fascist Germany and Yugoslavia or contemporary Poland. There is nothing, absolutely nothing in the past of Marxism to prevent a Marxist saying that in its death-agony, capitalism, though in its classic form an economy of private property, can reach a stage where the capitalist class can plan the economy as a whole. This would have been a great triumph for our movement, so well laid were the foundations and *the method* in the past. But our ancestors could say this because Marx, Engels, Lenin, Bukharin, took it as a corollary that centralization meant the intensification of the crisis for such a capitalism.

But up to 1919 this was not the issue. Bukharin's theory of state-capitalism is not ours, and was criticized even in his own day, but he elaborated it in the *ABC of Communism*; the book was highly praised by Lenin and was sold in millions of copies and several languages as an official party textbook. Why? Because he wrote that even if anarchy of individual capitalism was abrogated by state-capitalism, collapse was still inevitable. *Had he written the opposite* the denunciations would have started with Lenin.

That was Bolshevism. And that was how Trotsky wrote in the *First Manifesto of the Communist International*: "The state control of social life against which capitalist liberalism so strived, is to become a reality. There is no turning back either to free competition or to the domination of trusts, syndicates, and other kinds of social anomalies. The question consists solely in this: who shall control state production in the future—the imperialist state or the state of the victorious proletariat?"

To this 1919 analysis of Trotsky's, "Johnson-Forest" still subscribe wholeheartedly.

Pablo and State-Capitalism

It is obvious (and this is only a small selection of the material) that the whole past of our movement made it difficult to escape the theoretical possibility that Russia might be a form of state-capitalism. The Stalinist theoreticians knew all this. There had been restlessness in Russia over it. (No such restlessness stirred the majority of Trotskyists, secure in the belief that the nationalized property rendered all such considerations useless.) But—once Pablo *decided* on the road he was following, he recognized state-capitalism as the enemy. He warns against it repeatedly, warns Germain that that is where he will end, and undertakes at last to explain it.

Pablo explains that when Engels wrote about state-capitalism he was "like Trotsky . . . referring to the tendency." This is a positive crime. Trotsky and Engels were here at opposite poles. Trotsky writes: "State-capitalism means the substitution of state-property for private property and for that very reason remains partial in character." Engels writes: "Taking over of the great institutions for production and communication, first by joint-stock companies, later on by trusts, then by the State."[1]

What did Pablo expect Engels to write: "Taking over of the great institutions of production, each and every single one, by which I mean omitting none, etc., etc."?

Pablo continues: "Engels in that day little suspected the enormous concentration of monopoly capitalism which followed his epoch."

Engels spoke continually of trusts, trusts, trusts. Lenin and others constantly referred to Engels' analysis of trusts, trusts, trusts. In the quotation already cited, Engels says, "trusts which command and monopolize entire branches of industry." Pablo flips the great achievements of Marxism into the dustbin. What fanaticism is this? "Johnson-Forest" have met it before, in the Shachtmanites. When faced with questions

---

1   Engels writes this in a supplement to the chapters from *Anti-Dühring*, which he reprinted in *Socialism: Scientific and Utopian*. No one so far, not even the Stalinists as far as we know, has ever denied that the original statements in *Anti-Dühring* theoretically take the question to complete state-ownership.

like these, their attitude always was: Tear down the skies; root up the foundations; let everything go to ruin rather than accept this simple fact: No rearrangement of capital on capital's side of the barricades, actual or to the furthest degree of theoretical possibility, can solve the contradictions of capitalism which remain the exclusive task of the revolutionary proletariat.

Who opposes Pablo? All we have seen so far is some Shachtmanesque leaps and jumps by Germain. In *The Invading Socialist Society* (24) we quoted Lenin and prodded Germain. No answer.

Now suddenly, life having destroyed his theory, characteristically Trotskyist, that only the masses could nationalize property in Eastern Europe, and under pressure by Pablo, Germain announces in portentous language and big print:

> We are confronted by *transitional* cases, cases of combined development, in which the property relations can be overturned without the economy thereby automatically becoming an economy orienting away from capitalism toward socialism, and without permitting us to conclude that what we have is a workers' state. (*The Yugoslav Question, the Question of the Buffer Zone, and their Implication for Marxist Theory*, 12)

IN THESE TRANSITIONAL SITUATIONS THE LAW OF COMBINED DEVELOPMENT CAN PRESENT CASES IN WHICH THE STATIFICATION OF THE GREATEST PART OF THE MEANS OF PRODUCTION AND EXCHANGE CAN BE THE WORK OF A NON-WORKERS' STATE. IN SUCH SITUATIONS, THIS STATIFICATION THEN CEASES TO BE AN *AUTOMATIC CRITERION* PROVING THE EXISTENCE OF A WORKERS' STATE. (Ibid., 14)

This is the theory of exceptionalism so devastated by Trotsky, transferred to the whole world. In passing it gives the same treatment to the economic basis of the Trotskyist theory of state-property that Pablo gives to Engels, throws it on the dust heap. Who accepts this, who does not accept this, we do not know. If this is not chaos, we are willing to use any other word which is suggested to us.

Varga and State-Capitalism

No such confusion is tolerated near the Stalinists. For a brief period, when it seemed they were uncertain of their relation with Western Europe, they themselves called the states in Eastern Europe state-capitalism. Even they recognized that they were either workers' states or state-capitalism, even *they*. Then when the line turned, they went straight back to Leontiev in 1943. This is what is falsely known as the Varga controversy around Varga's book *Changes in the Political Economy of Capitalism Resulting from the Second World War*. It was not Varga alone. It was practically the whole staff of the Institute of World Economics which he headed. Faced with the fact that capitalism had not collapsed, Varga was the mouthpiece of the Institute which could find a reason for the continued existence of capitalism only in the fact that capitalism moved to state-capitalism, which could plan.

Varga was more careful than Pablo because he at least said that this equilibrium would last for a decade and not for centuries. His economic theory was also superior to Pablo's. For at the same time, along with his underconsumptionism, Varga, the mouthpiece, very cautiously reintroduced the theory of the falling rate of profit, holding it so to speak in reserve against his previous underconsumptionism. Despite the caution, these statements by Varga showed that the Stalinists know very well how to analyze state-capitalism and the falling rate of profit.

When the turn came, the reaction was brutal. In the course of the discussion on Varga's book one bold woman, Maria Natavno Smit, attacked Varga from the Left: "The book," she began, "lacks an analysis of the great new change connected with the transition from simple monopoly capitalism to state-monopoly capitalism, as Lenin understood this transition."

She then proceeded to quote Lenin: "During the war, world capitalism took a step forward not only toward concentration in general, but also toward state-capitalism in even a greater degree than formerly" (*Collected Works*, Russian ed., XXX, 300).

Smit concluded: "Where Lenin unites the concept of 'state' and of monopoly, Comrade Varga seems to separate them; each exists by itself and meanwhile, in fact, the process of coalescence of the state with monopoly manifests itself quite sharply at the present time in such countries as the U.S.A. and England."

It was an attempt to start where Lenin had left off, and by his method to deal with the vast experiences of thirty years. She was stamped down at once. "Imperialism is what Lenin elucidates. This is the stage of decay and death of capitalism, beyond which no new phase of capitalism follows.... I think one should agree with Comrade Varga who does not seek such a phase and does not try to establish a transition to such a phase."[2]

And this "new phase" would be what? Nothing else but state-capitalism. They know that Lenin's whole method prepared for this and nothing else but this.

Varga in his turn said that Smit "tried to advance a new theoretical idea," and that "the question is one of terminology and not one of substance."

Leninism and with it the theory of state-capitalism was buried once more.

The outline is necessarily summary. It is not the fault of "Johnson-Forest" if we have, in 1950, to spend so much space and time on what should be elementary questions in this discussion. But if we do not do it, who else will? We have said enough to show how profoundly state-capitalism and everything connected with it is embedded in the past and is today in the center of the arena and of the crises in Stalinist political economy. And the Fourth International? A blank, a complete and comprehensive blank! Worse. Every word it writes *fortifies* Stalinism.

---

2   The stenographic transcript of the entire discussion was published in English by Public Affairs Press, Washington, DC.

IV
Rearming the Party for the World Revolution

THE DIFFERENCES BETWEEN the Third International and the Fourth must be seen first as profoundly antagonistic theories of sociology, of accumulation, of capitalist collapse, of planned economy, of what constitutes bureaucracy, of what constitutes the party—a totally different methodology which *in the end* amounts to the aims and methods of different classes. "Johnson-Forest" are confident that our theory presents such an opposition to Stalinism.

We shall analyze and confront these two point by point. And each time we shall also show how inadequate is the theory of the Fourth International as an opposition to Stalinism.

1. (a) Stalinist sociology rests on the theory that the conversion of private property into state-property is the conversion of capitalism into socialism.

(b) The Fourth International must oppose to this that the basis of socialism is the emancipation of the proletariat from enslavement to capital, i.e., soviet power, the state power in the hands of the proletariat in its own proletarian organizations. This and this alone constitutes socialism, a new society, and a new state, or a transition to a new society.

(c) Trotsky denied absolutely that it was possible for private property to be concentrated into the hands of the state except by proletarian revolution.[1] He put state-property on the proletarian side of the barricades. On this proposition Trotsky was wrong but not confused.

---

1   On this Hansen and E.R. Frank have said all that is necessary and cannot be answered. They are striving to apply the doctrine they have been brought up on. That is why they are so wrong.

(d) Today, however, on this simple but basic proposition, official Trotskyism shows a mass of equivocation and confusion which grows every hour and from which it is impossible to extract any guiding line whatever.

2. (a) The Stalinists claim today that the distinguishing characteristic of capitalism in contrast with socialism is anarchy of production due to individual appropriation based on private property. Therefore, according to them, the fundamental economic crisis of capitalism is due to ineffective demand, the inability of markets to absorb production. State-property abolishes these fundamental antagonisms of capitalism and thereby becomes a superior society which can *plan*.

(b) The Fourth International must show that the basic economic contradiction of capitalism is in production, the falling rate of profit. This a totally centralized capital cannot overcome.

(c) Trotsky obviously was familiar with this (the fundamental theoretical question of Marxian economics for two generations). He never committed himself to any *theory* of underconsumption. But his whole conception of the superiority of planned economy was based on the law of value as anarchy and the superiority of state-property because it and it alone allowed society to plan.

(d) Today the press of official Trotskyism is ridden with underconsumptionism. On the other hand, on the question of the capacity of centralized capital to plan, it is today impossible to get any guiding line, as witness the resolution of the IEC, as to why planning is impossible in the satellite countries, very properly exposed by Hansen. Germain does not know the difference between the falling rate of profit and the average rate of profit and by a not at all accidental fatality, he follows Leontiev in writing average rate of profit where he should write falling rate.

Pablo tells us that within a society with the "new property relations" of general statification, "the laws of capitalist economy operate in a changed fashion and not automatically or *blindly*" (*Yugoslavia and the Rest of the Buffer Zones*, 13, emphasis in original).[2] In the same bulletin he tells us that a capitalism which achieved complete statification would be a "*regenerated* capitalist state," and it would "mean considerable

---

2   This is precisely the revision in the Marxist analysis of the law of value which Leontiev introduced in 1943.

progress and in no sense a decline" (4). Just note, please, the phrase "in no sense a decline."

We have made it clear that, in harmony with all the great Marxists, we believe that capitalist planning does not in the slightest degree allow it to escape the laws of capitalism, which are at this stage intensified and irresistible. But observe, if you please, a leader of our movement, in this period, the death-agony of capitalism, can find laws of capitalism which, however, will show no decline. Observe, too, that nobody attacks him.

3. (a) The theory of Stalinism denies that the economic manifestation of the new society is the *qualitatively* increased productivity of labor. It substitutes instead as criterion the *quantitative* accumulation of goods, or growth of "the socialist sector," i.e., state-property. It sees the problems of Stalinist production exclusively as a problem of relations between means of production and means of consumption, a relation which it claims to control. This can be modified to the eventual advantage of the proletariat solely by increase of capital. The inequalities and sufferings of the Russian workers are, therefore, due to lack of consumption goods, the result of the need for accumulation.

Upon this basis the distinguishing feature of Stalinist production is the need for increase of norms and intensification of labor, an incessant hounding and driving of the workers in production in the name of increased accumulation. This is the Stalinist theory, refined and elaborated in a thousand documents.

(b) To this the Fourth International must oppose the view that the new productive system of socialism is primarily distinguished by an entirely new organization of labor *within the process of production itself*, in a reorganization of society beginning in the factory, the center of production relations, resulting in a form of labor that will as far surpass capitalism as capitalism surpassed feudalism. Marx's theory is based upon the fact that as long as production is carried on "within the conditions of production themselves by special agents in opposition to the direct producers," accumulated labor is in opposition to living labor; as it accumulates, misery accumulates, and the class struggle paralyzes productivity and production.

(c) Trotsky saw the strictly economic decline of capitalism in the fact that world capitalism could no longer quantitatively increase accumulation. This has been proved utterly false. All that this conspicuously false theory of accumulation does is to fortify the Stalinist contrast between the presumed incapacity of capitalism to accumulate and the presumed power of Russia to accumulate indefinitely.

Historically, i.e., concretely, the monopoly of capital is a "fetter" upon production. It is not an absolute barrier. Lenin vigorously denied that the stagnation of capitalism meant cessation of growth. The Marxist analysis is increase of conflict, of crisis and of degeneration, as a result of increase of growth.

Trotsky declared that the proletariat does not grow under world capitalism and declines in culture. This is absolutely false and is in direct opposition to the thesis of Marx that in the very crisis of capitalism the proletariat is "always increasing in numbers and is united, disciplined and organized," i.e., prepared socially for its tasks, by the very mechanism of capitalist production itself.

(d) Today with Russian production far beyond what it was in 1936, the year of *The Revolution Betrayed*, orthodox Trotskyism, as is shown in the World Congress Resolution of 1948, still teaches that the Stalinist barbarism is rooted in the struggle over consumption goods. This theory fails to expose the greatest crime in Russia, the monstrous daily persecution of millions of workers in the very process of production. It does more. It attributes the Stalinist state-power, the most monstrous in history, of more unbridled savagery than the state of German Fascism, it attributes all this to the struggle over consumption goods within the framework of a higher form of economy.

The Stalinists attribute any crisis in production in Russia to "remnants of capitalist ideology in the working class." Orthodox Trotskyism finds the remnants of capitalist ideology in the thieving bureaucracy. But the method is the same, subjectivism.

Sociology based upon form of property, i.e., relations between men and things, a theory of accumulation based upon consumption, socialism as the plan by which these inequalities of property and consumption are readjusted—this is the sociology, the economics and the politics of Stalinism inside and outside Russia.

Sociology based upon relations of production, that is to say, relations between people, a theory of accumulation based upon production, socialism as the organization of a higher mode of labor, that is the theory the International of world revolution must adopt. That is the theory of "Johnson-Forest," the theory of state-capitalism, Marxism of *our* period.

It is this theory which the Stalinists wish to destroy, root and branch, in every implication and manifestation. And that is not in the least surprising. What we call the theory of state-capitalism is the theory of the proletariat as a class directed against capital and any agent of capital, in this case the bureaucracy. Thus the difference between Stalinism and "Johnson-Forest" is a difference of *class*. Every line of Stalinist theory aims at the obliteration of the question of class in the theory and practice of what they call socialism. And regrettably, very regrettably, we shall have to show that the theories of the Fourth International have fortified the theories of Stalinism. The true significance of Pablo is that he has brought this that was implicit in the theories of the Fourth International out into the open.

V
The Class Struggle

THE STALINIST THEORY is, despite zigzags, logical and consistent. Like every theory of all exploiters it is the theory of the rulers, the result of their struggle with the direct producers whom they exploit, and of competition with other rulers. The theory justifies Stalinist exploitation of the Russian workers. It can be used as a weapon against the traditional bourgeoisie in the struggle for the domination of the world working class movement without impairing the position of the rulers inside Russia. It fortifies this position in the minds of the public which is interested in these questions and the members and fellow-travellers of the Stalinist parties.

The theory itself is an adaptation of the pre-Marxian petty-bourgeois ideology from Kant to Sismondi and Proudhon to the specific conditions of state-capitalism. That we shall go into later. But then as now its purpose can be summed up in a phrase—the radical reorganization of society with the proletariat as object and not as subject, i.e., with no essential change in the mode of labor. The crisis of world-capitalism, a hundred years of Marxism, thirty years of Leninism, impose upon this theory, as a primary task, the need to destroy and to obscure the theory of class struggle in the process of production itself, the very basis of Marxism and of the proletarian revolution.

The Stalinists did not arbitrarily "choose" this theory. Politics on the basis of the analysis of property is of necessity the struggle over correct policy and the correction of "evil." Social division, if not rooted in *classes*, automatically becomes a selection of personnel. The criterion not being a criterion of class becomes automatically a criterion according to competence, ability, loyalty, devotion, etc. This personnel, comprising many millions, the Stalinists have enshrined in the 1936 constitution under the name of "our socialist intelligentsia." The most competent, the most able, most loyal, most devoted, the elite become the party. The instrument of the party is the state. The corollary to disguising the rulers of production as "our socialist intelligentsia" is the Stalinist denunciation of bureaucracy as inefficiency, red tape, rudeness to workers, laziness, etc.—purely subjective characterizations.

The Bureaucracy in Industry

The first task of the revolutionary International is clarification of this term, bureaucracy. The Stalinists take advantage of the fact that Marx often used the term, bureaucracy, in relation to the mass of state functionaries. But with the analysis of state-capitalism by Engels, the word *bureaucracy* began to take on a wider connotation. Where Engels says "Taking over of the great institutions for production and communication, first by joint-stock companies, later on by trusts, then by the State," he adds: "The bourgeoisie demonstrated to be a superfluous class. All its social functions are now performed by salaried employees" (*Socialism, Utopian and Scientific*, 138). These are bureaucrats.

The moment Lenin saw the Soviet, the new form of social organization created by the masses, he began to extend the concept, bureaucracy, to include not only officials of government but the officials of industry, all who were opposed to the proletariat as masters. This appears all through *State and Revolution* and, in its most finished form, in the following:

> We cannot do without officials *under capitalism, under the rule of the bourgeoisie*. The proletariat is oppressed, the masses of the toilers are enslaved by capitalism. Under capitalism democracy is restricted, cramped, curtailed, mutilated by all the conditions of wage-slavery, the poverty and misery of the masses. This is why and the only reason why the officials of our political and industrial organizations are corrupted—or more precisely, tend to be corrupted—by the conditions of capitalism, why they betray a tendency to become transformed into bureaucrats, i.e., into privileged persons divorced from the masses and *superior to* the masses.

This is the *essence* of bureaucracy, and until the capitalists have been expropriated and the bourgeoisie overthrown, *even* proletarian officials will inevitably be "bureaucratized" to some extent.

Lenin's whole strategic program between July and October is based upon the substitution of the power of the armed masses for the power of the bureaucrat, the master, the official in industry and in politics. Hence his reiterated statement that if you nationalize and even confiscate, it means nothing without workers' power. Just as he had extended the analysis of capitalism, to state-capitalism and plan, Lenin was developing the theory of class struggle in relation to the development of capitalism itself. This strengthened the basic concepts of Marxism.

Marx says:

> The authority assumed by the capitalist by his personification of capital in the direct process of production, the social function performed by him in his capacity as a manager and ruler of production, is essentially different from the authority exercised upon the basis of production by means of slaves, serfs, etc.
>
> Upon the basis of capitalist production, the social character of their production impresses itself upon the mass of direct producers as a strictly regulating authority and as a social mechanism of the labor process graduated into a complete hierarchy. This authority is vested in its bearers only as a personification of the requirements of labor standing above the laborer. (*Capital*, Vol. III, 1027)

This is capitalist production, this hierarchy. The special functions are performed "within the conditions of production themselves by special agents in opposition to the direct producers" (1025). These functionaries, acting against the proletariat in production, are the enemy. If this is not understood, workers' control of production is an empty phrase.

With the development of capitalism into state-capitalism, as far back as 1917, Lenin, in strict theory, denounced mere confiscation in order to concentrate his whole fire upon the hierarchy in the process of production itself, and to counterpose to this, workers' power. It thus becomes ever more clear why the Stalinists in their theory will have nothing whatever to do with state-capitalism and rebuke and stamp out any suggestions of it so sharply. The distinction that Lenin always kept clear has now developed with the development of capitalism over the last thirty years. It has now grown until it becomes the dividing line between the workers and the whole bureaucratic organization of accumulated labor, science and knowledge, acting against the working class in the immediate process of production and everywhere else. This is the sense in which the term bureaucracy must be used in Russia.

"A Higher Social Organization of Labor"

It is upon this Leninist *analysis* that the theory of state-capitalism rests, and inseparable from this theory, the concept of the *transition* from social labor as compulsion, as barracks discipline of capital, to social labor as the voluntary association, the voluntary labor discipline of the laborers themselves. Lenin in "The Great Beginning" theoretically and practically wrote an analysis of labor in Russia which the development of society *on a world scale* during the last thirty years, now raises to the highest position among all his work on Russia. This must be the foundation of a Marxist approach to the problems of economics and politics under socialism. In that article Lenin did two things:

(a) Established with all the emphasis at his command that the essential character of the dictatorship of the proletariat was "not violence and not mainly violence against the exploiters." It was the unity and discipline of the proletariat trained by capitalism, its ability to produce "a higher social organization of labor."

(b) Analyzed the Communist days of labor given to the Soviet state and sought to distinguish the specific social and psychological characteristics of a new form of labor, and the relation of that to the productivity of labor.

With all its mighty creations of a Soviet state and Red Army, and the revolution in the superstructure, it is here that the Russian socialist revolution could not be completed. The "historical creative initiative" in production, the "subtle and intricate" relations of a new labor process—these never developed for historical reasons. But there has been a vast development of capitalism and of the understanding of capitalism all over the world since the early days of the Russian Revolution. The British Chancellor of the Exchequer, the Stalinist bureaucracy, the whole capitalist class in the U.S. (and in the U.S. more than anywhere else)—all declare that the problem of production today is the productivity of labor and the need to harness the human interest, i.e., the energy and ability of the worker. Many of them are aware that it is the labor process itself which is in question.

What they see partially, contemporary Marxism must see fully and thereby restore the very foundations of Marxism as a social science.

It is in the concrete analysis of labor inside Russia and outside Russia that the Fourth International can find the basis of the profoundest difference between the Third International and the Fourth International. The whole tendency of the Stalinist theory is to build up theoretical barriers between the Russian economy and the economy of the rest of the world. The task of the revolutionary movement, beginning in theory and as we shall see, reaching to all aspects of political strategy, is to break down this separation. The development of Russia is to be explained by the development of world capitalism and specifically, capitalist production in its most advanced stage, in the United States. Necessary for the strategic task of clarifying its own theory and for building an irreconcilable opposition to Stalinism, it is not accidental that this method also is the open road for the revolutionary party to the socialism inherent in the minds and hearts, not only of the politically advanced but the most backward industrial workers in the United States.

It is for this reason that the analysis of the labor process in the United States must concern us first and only afterwards the labor process in Stalinist Russia.

The Mode of Labor in the United States

Roughly, we may attribute the decisive change in the American economy to the last part of the nineteenth century and the first part of the twentieth century, taking 1914 as a convenient dividing line. After World War I the Taylor system, experimental before the war, becomes a social system, the factory laid out for continuous flow of production, and advanced planning for production, operating and control. At the same time there is the organization of professional societies, management courses in college curricula and responsible management consultants. Between 1924 and 1928 there is rationalization of production and retooling (Ford).[1] Along with it are the tendencies to the scientific organization of production, to closer coordination between employers, fusion with each other against the working class, the intervention of the state as mediator and then as arbiter.

For the proletariat there is the constantly growing subdivision of labor, decrease in the need of skills, and determination of the sequence of operations and speed by the machine. The crisis of 1929 accelerated all these processes. The characteristic, most advanced form of American production becomes Ford. Here production consists of a mass of hounded, sweated labor (in which, in Marx's phrase, the very life of society was threatened); and opposed to it as a class, a management staff which can carry out this production only by means of a hired army (Bennett) of gangsters, thugs, supervisors who run production by terror, in the plant, in the lives of the workers outside production, and in the political control of Detroit. Ford's regime before unionization is the prototype of production relations in Fascist Germany and Stalinist Russia.

But—and without this, *all* Marxism is lost—inextricably intertwined with the totalitarian *tendency* is the response of the working class. A whole new layer of workers, the result of the economic development, burst into revolt in the CIO. The CIO in its inception aimed at a revolution in production. The workers would examine what they were told to do and then decide whether it was satisfactory to them or not. This rejection of the basis of capitalist economy is the preliminary basis of a socialist economy. The next positive step is the total management of industry by the proletariat. Where the *Transitional Program* says that the "CIO is the most indisputable expression of the instinctive striving of the American workers to raise themselves to the level of the tasks imposed upon them by history," it is absolutely correct. The task imposed upon them by history is socialism and the outburst, in aim and method, was the first instinctive preparation of the social revolution.

Because it was not and could not be carried through to a conclusion, the inevitable counterpart was the creation of a labor bureaucracy. The

---

1   A similar process in Germany led straight to Hitler.

history of production since is the corruption of the bureaucracy and its transformation into an instrument of capitalist production, the restoration to the bourgeoisie of what it had lost in 1936, the right to control production standards. Without this mediating role of the bureaucracy, production in the United States would be violently and continuously disrupted until one class was undisputed master.

The whole system is in mortal crisis from the reaction of the workers. Ford, whose father fought the union so uncompromisingly as late as 1941, now openly recognizes that as far as capitalism is concerned, improvements in technology, i.e., the further mechanization of labor, offers no road out for the increase of productivity which rests entirely with the working class. At the same time, the workers in relation to capitalism resist any increase in productivity. The resistance to speed-up does not necessarily mean as most think that workers are required to work beyond normal physical capacity. It is resistance by the workers to any increased productivity, i.e., any increase of productivity by capitalist methods. Thus, both sides, capital and labor, are animated by the fact that for each, in its own way, the system has reached its limit.

The real aim of the great strikes in 1946 and since is the attempt to begin on a higher stage what was initiated in 1936. But the attempt is crippled and deflected by the bureaucracy, with the result that rationalization of production, speed-up, intensification of exploitation are the order of the day in industry.

The bureaucracy inevitably must substitute the struggle over consumption, higher wages, pensions, education, etc., for a struggle in production. This is the basis of the welfare state, the attempt to appease the workers with the fruits of labor when they seek satisfaction in the work itself. The bureaucracy must raise a new social program in the realm of consumption because it cannot attack capitalism at the point of production without destroying capitalism itself.

The series of pension plans which have now culminated in the five-year contract with General Motors is a very sharp climax of the whole struggle. This particular type of increase in consumption subordinates the workers to production in a special manner after they have reached a certain age. It confines them to being an industrial reserve army, not merely at the disposal of capital in general but within the confining limits of the specific capitalist factory which employs them. The effect, therefore, is to reinforce control both of employers and bureaucracy over production.

But along with this intensification of capitalist production and this binding of the worker for five years *must* go inevitably the increase of revolt, wildcat strikes, a desperate attempt of the working class to gain for itself conditions of labor that are denied to it both by the employers and the labor bureaucracy. While the bureaucracy provides the leadership for struggles over consumption, it is from the workers on the line that emerges the initiative for struggles over speed-up. That is precisely why the bureaucracy, after vainly trying to stop wildcat strikes by prohibiting them in the contract, has now taken upon itself the task of repressing by force this interruption of production. It expels from the unions workers who indulge in these illegal stoppages, i.e., who protest against the present stage of capitalist production itself. The flying squads, originated by the union for struggle against the bourgeoisie, are now converted by the bureaucracy into a weapon of struggle against the proletariat, and all this in the name of a higher standard of living, greater consumption by the workers, but in reality to ensure capitalist production.

The increase of coercion and terror by the bureaucracy increases the tendency of the workers to violent explosion. This tendency, taken to its logical conclusion, as the workers will have to take it, means the reorganization of the whole system of production itself—socialism. Either this or the complete destruction of the union movement as the instrument of proletarian emancipation and its complete transformation into the only possible instrument of capital against the proletariat at this stage of production.

This is the fundamental function of the bureaucracy *in Russia*. Already the tentative philosophy of the bureaucracy in the United States, its political economy of regulation of wages and prices, nationalization and even planning, its ruthless political methods, show the organic similarity of the American labor bureaucracy and the Stalinists. The struggle in the United States reveals concretely what is involved in the Stalinist falsification of the Marxist theory of accumulation, etc., and the totalitarian violence against the proletariat which this falsification protects.

In the recent coal strikes, despite the wage and welfare gains of the miners, the heads of the operators declared that control of production had been restored to them by the two-year contract. C.E. Wilson, president of General Motors, hailed the five-year settlement as allowing the company "to run our own plants," and as "the union's complete acceptance of technological progress." Reuther hailed the G.M. settlement as a "tremendous step forward" in "stabilizing labor relations at G.M." An editor of *Fortune* magazine hailed the contract as the harbinger of "new and more meaningful associative principles" with the corporation as "the center of a new kind of community."

The Stalinist bureaucracy is the American bureaucracy carried to its ultimate and logical conclusion, both of them products of capitalist production in the epoch of state-capitalism. To reply to this that the bureaucracy can never arrive at maturity without a proletarian revolution is the complete degradation of Marxist theory. Not a single Marxist of all the great Marxists who analyzed state-capitalism, not one ever believed capitalism would reach the specific stage of complete centralization. It was because of the necessity to examine all its tendencies in order to be able to mobilize theoretical and practical opposition in the proletariat that they followed the dialectical method and *took these tendencies to their conclusions as an indispensable theoretical step*. In the present stage of our theory it is the scrupulous analysis of production in the United States as the most advanced stage of world capitalism that forms the indispensable prelude to the analysis of the labor process of Russia.

The Mode of Labor in Russia

The Russian Revolution of October 1917 abolished feudalism with a thoroughness never before achieved. The stage was therefore set for a tremendous economic expansion. Lenin sought to mobilize the proletariat to protect itself from being overwhelmed by this economic expansion. The isolated proletariat of backward Russia was unable to do this. The subsequent history of the labor process of Russia is the telescopic re-enactment of the stages of the process of production of the United States; and, added to this, the special degradation imposed upon it by the totalitarian control of the bureaucracy and the plan.

The Russian Revolution in 1917 substituted for the authority of the capitalist in the factory the *workers' control of production*. Immediately there appeared *both* the concrete development of self-initiative in the factory *and* the simplification of the state apparatus outside. There was workers' control, with some capitalists as owners, but *mere* owners. Production conferences, not of bureaucrats but of workers, decided what and how to produce. What capitalists there remained seemed to vanish into thin air once their economic power was broken, and workers' control was supplemented the following year by nationalization of the means of production. The red thread that runs through these first years of workers' rule, workers' control, seems to suffer a setback under war communism in general and with order 1042 in particular.[2] It takes less than a year for the workers to force a change, and the all-important trade union debate of 1920 follows. Lenin fights successfully both Trotsky, the administrator, and Shlapnikov, the syndico-anarchist, and strives to steer a course in consonance with the Declaration of the Rights of the Toilers, that only the masses "from below" can manage the economy, and that the trade unions are the transmission belts to the state wherein "every cook can be an administrator."

Stalinism in the Russian Factory

In the transition period between 1924 and 1928 when the First Five-Year Plan is initiated, the production conferences undergo a bureaucratization, and with it the form of labor. There begins the alienation of mass activity to conform to specified quantities of *abstract labor* demanded by the Plan "to catch up with capitalism."

The results are:

(a) In 1929 ("The year of decision and transformation") there crystallizes in direct opposition to management by the masses "from below" the *conference of the planners*, the engineers, economists, administrators; in a word, the specialists.

---

2   This was the order issued in the attempt to get the completely disorganized railroad system to function. The railroads were placed under almost military rule, subordinating the ordinary trade union democracy to "Chief Political Departments" which were established in the railway and water transport workers' unions. As soon as the critical situation had been solved, the transport workers demanded the abolition of the "Chief Political Departments" and the immediate restoration of full trade union democracy.

(b) Stalin's famous talk of 1931 "put an end to depersonalization." His "six conditions" of labor contrasted the masses to the "personalized" individual who would outdo the *norms of the average*. Competition is not on the basis of creativity and Subbotniks, but on the basis of the outstanding individual (read: bureaucrat) who will devise norms and have others surpass them.[3]

(c) 1935 sees Stakhanovism and the definitive formation of an aristocracy of labor. Stakhanovism is the pure model of the manner in which foremen, overseers and leadermen are chosen in the factories the world over. These individuals, exceptional to their class, voluntarily devote an intensity of their labor to capital for a brief period, thus setting the norm, which they personify, to dominate the labor of the mass for an indefinite period.

With the Stakhanovites, the bureaucratic administrators acquire a social base, and alongside, there grows the instability and crisis in the economy. It is the counter-revolution of state-capital.

(d) Beginning with 1939 the mode of labor changes again. In his report on the Third Five-Year Plan, Molotov stressed the fact that it was insufficient to be concerned merely with the mass of goods produced. The crucial point for "outstripping capitalism" was *not the mass* but the *rate* at which that mass was produced. It was necessary that per capita production be increased, that is to say, that each worker's productivity be so increased that fewer workers would be needed to obtain an ever greater mass of goods. Intensity of labor becomes the norm.

During the war that norm turned out to be the most vicious of all forms of exploitation. The Stalinists sanctified it by the name of "socialist emulation." "Socialist emulation" meant, firstly, that the pay incentive that was the due of a Stakhanovite was no longer the reward of the workers as individuals, once they *as a mass* produced according to the new raised norm. In other words, the take-home pay was the same despite the speed-up on a plant-wide basis. Secondly, and above all, competition was no longer limited to individual workers competing on a

---

3   Subbotniks were the workers who on their own initiative volunteered to work five hours' overtime on Saturdays without pay in order to help the economy of the workers' state. From the word "Subbota," meaning Saturday.

piecework basis, nor even to groups of workers on a plant-wide basis, but was extended to cover *factory against factory*.

Labor Reserves are established to assure the perpetuation of skills and a sufficient labor supply. Youth are trained from the start to *labor as ordered*. The climax comes in 1943 with the "discovery" of the conveyor belt system. This is the year also of the Stalinist admission that the law of value functions in Russia.

We thus have:

1918: The Declaration of the Rights of Toilers—*every* cook an administrator.

1928: *Abstract* mass labor—"lots" of it "to catch up with capitalism."

1931: Differentiation within labor—"personalized" individual; the pieceworker the hero.

1935: Stakhanovism, *individual competition* to surpass the norm.

1936–37: Stalinist Constitution: Stakhanovites and the intelligentsia *singled out* as those "whom we respect."

1939–41: *Systematization* of piecework; factory competing against factory.

1943: "The year of the conversion to the conveyor belt system."

Whereas in 1936 we had the singling out of a ruling class, a "simple" division between mental and physical work, we now have the *stratification* of mental and physical labor. Leontiev's *Political Economy in the Soviet Union* lays stress not merely on the intelligentsia against the mass, but on specific skills and differentials, lower, higher, middle, in-between and highest.

If we take production since the Plan, not in the detail we have just given, but only the major changes, we can say that 1937 closes one period. It is the period of "catching up with and outdistancing capitalism" which means mass production and relatively simple planning. But competition on a *world* scale and the approaching Second World War is the severest type of capitalist competition for world mastery. This opens up the new period of per capita production as against mere "catching up." Planning must now include productivity of labor. Such planning knows and can know only machines and *intensity* of exploitation. Furthermore, it includes what the Russians call *rentabl'nost*, that is to say profitability. The era of the state helping the factory whose production is especially needed is over. The factory itself must prove its worthiness by showing a profit and a profit big enough to pay for "*ever-expanded*" production. And that can be done only by ever-expanded production of abstract labor in mass *and in rate*.

Nowhere in the world is labor so degraded as in Russia today. We are here many stages beyond the degradation which Marx described in the General Law of Accumulation. For not merely is the Russian laborer reduced to an appendage to a machine and a mere cog in the accumulation of capital. Marx said that the reserve army kept the working laborer riveted to his martyrdom. In Russia, because of the power to plan, the industrial reserve army is planned. Some fifteen million laborers are planned in direct forced labor camps. They are organized by the MVD (GPU) for production. The disciplinary laws which began with reduction in wages for coming fifteen minutes late have as their final stage, for lack of discipline, "corrective labor," i.e., the concentration camp.

What the American workers are revolting against since 1936 and holding at bay, this, and nothing else but this, has overwhelmed the Russian proletariat. The rulers of Russia perform the same functions as are performed by Ford, General Motors, the coal operators and their huge bureaucratic staffs. Capital is not Henry Ford; he can die and leave his whole empire to an institution; the plant, the scientific apparatus, the method, the personnel of organization and supervision, the social system which sets these up in opposition to the direct producer will remain. Not inefficiency of bureaucrats, not "prestige, powers and revenue of the bureaucracy," not consumption but capital accumulation in its specifically capitalist manner, this is the analysis of the Russian economy.

To think that the struggle in Russia is over consumption not only strikes at the whole theory of the relationship of the superstructure to the productive mechanism. In practice, today, the crisis in Russia is manifestly the crisis in production. Whoever is convinced that this whole problem is a problem of consumption is driven away from Marxism, not toward it.

The Crisis of State-Capitalism

It was Marx's contention that the existence of a laboring force compelled to sell its labor-power in order to live meant automatically the system of capitalist accumulation. The capitalist was merely the agent of capital. The bureaucrats are the same. Neither can use nor knows any other mode of production. A new mode of production requires primarily that they be totally removed or totally subordinated.

At this point, it is convenient to summarize briefly the abstract economic analysis of state-capitalism. We have never said that the economy of the United States is the same as the economy of Russia. What we have said is that, however great the differences, the fundamental laws of capitalism operate. It is just this that Marx indicated with his addition to *Capital* dealing with complete centralization of capital "in a given country."

"A given country" meant one specific country, i.e., the laws of the world-market still exist. If the whole world became centralized, then there would be a new society (for those who want it) since the *world-market* would have been destroyed. Although *completely centralized* capital "in a given country" can plan, it cannot plan away the contradictions of capitalist production. If the *organic composition* of capital on a world scale is 5 to 1, moving to 6 to 1, to 7 to 1, etc., centralized capital in a given country *has to keep pace with that.* The only way to escape it would be by a productivity of labor so great that it could keep ahead of the rest and still organize its production for use. Such a productivity of labor is impossible in capitalism which knows only the law of value and its consequence, accumulated labor and sweating proletarians. That is precisely why Engels wrote that though formally, i.e., abstractly, complete state-property could overcome the contradictions, actually it could not, the "workers remain proletarians." The whole long dispute between underconsumption and rate of profit theorists has now been definitively settled precisely by the experience of Russia.

Lenin in 1917 repeated that state-capitalism without the Soviets meant "military penal labor" for the workers. The Soviet power was the road to socialism. The struggle in Russia and outside is the struggle against "military penal labor" and for the Soviet power. The revolt which gave birth to the CIO prevented American capital from transforming the whole of American production and society into the system which Ford and Bennett had established. This monstrous burden would have driven capital still further along the road of accumulation of capital, domination over the direct producer or accumulation of misery, lowered productivity, barbarism, paralysis and gangrene in all aspects of society. That was Germany. That would be the plan, the plan of capital, and with state-property it is more free than before to plan its own ruin.

The totalitarian state in Russia prevents the workers from making their social and political experiences in open class struggle. But by so doing, it ensures the unchecked reign of capital, the ruin of production and society, and the inevitability of total revolution.

The decisive question is not whether centralization is complete or partial, heading toward completeness. The vital necessity of our time is to lay bare the violent antagonism of labor and capital at this definitive stage of centralization of capital. Whether democratic or totalitarian, both types of society are in permanent decline and insoluble crisis. Both are at a stage when only a total reorganization of social relations can lift society a stage higher. It is noteworthy that in the United States the capitalist class is aware of this, and the most significant work that is being done in political economy is the desperate attempt to find some way of reconciling the working class to the agonies of mechanized production and transferring its implacable resistance into creative cooperation. That is of educational value and many of its findings will be used by the socialist proletariat. In Russia this resistance is labeled "remnants of capitalist ideology" and the whole power of the totalitarian state is organized to crush it in theory as well as in fact.

We shall see that upon this theoretical analysis the whole strategy of revolutionary politics is qualitatively differentiated from Stalinism, inside and outside Russia. The Stalinists seek to establish themselves in the place of the rival bureaucracy. The rival bureaucracy seeks to substitute itself in the place of Stalinism. The Fourth International must not seek to substitute itself for either of these, not after, not during nor before the conquest of power. Theory and practice are governed by the recognition of the necessity that the bureaucracy as such must be overthrown.

The Bureaucratic Administrative Plan

We can now come to a theoretical conclusion about the question of plan and with it, nationalization. For the capitalist mode of labor in its advanced stages, the bureaucratic administrative plan can become the greatest instrument of torture for the proletariat that capitalism has yet produced. State-property and total planning are nothing else but the complete subordination of the proletariat to capital. That is why in *The Invading Socialist Society* we summed up our total theory in two points, the first of which is:

> 1. IT IS THE TASK OF THE FOURTH INTERNATIONAL TO DRIVE AS CLEAR A LINE BETWEEN BOURGEOIS NATION- ALIZATION AND PROLETARIAN NATIONALIZATION AS THE REVOLUTIONARY THIRD INTERNATIONAL DROVE BETWEEN BOURGEOIS DEMOCRACY AND PROLETARIAN DEMOCRACY.

All theory for our epoch must begin here.

But aren't state-property and the plan progressive? State-property as such and plan as such are metaphysical abstractions. They have a class content. Aren't trusts progressive, Lenin was asked in 1916. He replied:

> It is the work of the bourgeoisie to develop trusts, to drive children and women into factories, to torture them there, corrupt them and condemn them to the utmost misery. We do not "demand" such a development; we do not "support" it; we struggle against it. But *how* do we struggle? We know that trusts and factory work of women are progressive. We do not wish to go backwards to crafts, to premonopolist capitalism, to domestic work of women. Forward through the trusts, etc., and beyond them toward socialism! (*The Bolsheviks and the World War*, 495)

We reply similarly. This is Marxism—the antagonism of classes. Under capitalism, private or state, all science, knowledge, organization, are developed only at the expense and degradation of the proletariat. But at the same time capitalism organizes the proletariat for struggle. We do not "demand" or "support" plan. We propose to substitute proletarian power and subordinate plan to the revolutionary struggle of the proletariat.

Where does orthodox Trotskyism stand on this? Every member knows the answer. Nowhere. Its conception of plan is summarized in the slogan in the *Transitional Program*: "The plan must be revised from top to bottom in the interests of the producers and consumers."

The capitalist plan cannot be revised except in the interests of capital. It is not the plan that is to be revised. It is the whole mode of production which is to be overthrown.

The whole analysis is in terms of (to use the underlined phrases of the *Transitional Program*) "*social inequality*" and "*political inequality.*" In *The Revolution Betrayed* the chapter entitled "The Struggle for Productivity of Labor" deals with money and plan, inflation, rehabilitation of the ruble. It says that analysis of Stakhanovism proves that it is a vicious form of piecework. But it soon returns to the question of the ruble. And it finally ends on the note that the Soviet administrative personnel is "far less adequate to the productive tasks than the workers." Therefore, what is needed is more competence, more efficiency, less red tape, less laziness, etc. If the Russian bureaucracy were more efficient, more scientific, etc., the results for the Russian proletariat would be worse.

The chapter "Social Relations in the Soviet Union" in *The Revolution Betrayed* deals with the privileges, wages, etc. of the bureaucracy in relation to the workers. Neither in the *Transitional Program* nor *The Revolution Betrayed* does analysis of the worker in the production process find any place, except where in the *Program* the slogan is raised, "Factory committees should be returned the right to control production." In the analyses of orthodox Trotskyism there are a few references here and there to creative initiative being needed at this stage. That is all.

All the slogans in the *Transitional Program* do nothing more than demand the restoration of democracy to where it was in 1917, thereby showing that the whole great experience of thirty years has passed orthodox Trotskyism by. World capitalism has moved to the crisis and counter-revolution in production. The program for the reintroduction of political democracy does no more than reintroduce the arena for the reintroduction of a new bureaucracy when the old one is driven out.

But, after all, production relations must include somewhere workers, labor, the labor process—the place where the population is differentiated by function. The World Congress Resolution (*Fourth International*, June 1948) quotes from *The Revolution Betrayed* an elaborate summary by Trotsky of his own position in 1936. The worker in the labor process is not mentioned. The resolution asks: What alterations have to be made in the analysis following the development of the past eleven years? It begins: "the social differentiation is the result of bourgeois norms of *distribution*; it has not yet entered the domain of ownership of the means of production."

The struggle out of which the CIO was born, the domination of the machine, the drive for greater productivity, what about that? The Orthodox Trotskyist in 1950 would have to reply: the question is not a question of production. It is a question of collective ownership; it is a question of the thieving bureaucracy taking for itself consumption goods which belong to the workers; it is a question of whether the bureaucracy passes laws of inheritance; it is a question in 1950 as it was in 1934 of whether the tendency to primitive accumulation will restore private property, etc., etc. Is this an injustice to Orthodox Trotskyism? If it is, then *what* would it reply, and where is any other reply to be found?

VI
The Theory of the Party

(A) THE STALINIST theory and practice of the party is the direct result of the Stalinist conception of Plan. The party consists of the elite, the most efficient, the most loyal, the most devoted, etc. The party mobilizes the proletariat, politically, economically and morally, *to carry out the Plan*. There is here no parallel with the political parties and politics of capitalist competition and bourgeois democracy. In state-capitalism the state becomes capitalistic in the sense of administration, supervision, control against the proletariat. The party forms the state in its own image, which is the reflection of the productive process of state-capitalism. That was the party of Hitler (despite historical differences), that is the party of Stalin.

The Stalinist parties outside Russia function on the same model. Their attitude to the membership and the proletariat is that of an elite leading backward workers. All initiative, policy, direction comes from the Stalinist leaders. Society will be saved if it follows them, defends them, puts its trust in them. Historical circumstances may alter their practice, but in their fundamental conceptions there is no difference whatever between the CP in Russia and the CP in the United States.

(b) Upon the basis of its analysis of state-capitalism and Plan, the Leninist party must form its own revolutionary theory of the party. The party is, in Lenin's words, based upon the factory but upon the progressive cooperation aspect of the factory: unity, discipline and organization of the working class, in unalterable opposition to the theory and practice of the elite.

Every age has its own specific development of production and its specific social relations. *Each* separate International has its own separate (and antagonistic) conception of the party which is rooted in *its own* social base and its conception of its political tasks in relation to that base. Marx's conception of the party in 1848, the way he organized the

First International, carefully explained by him; the organization of the Second International which Lenin accepted as sound up to 1914; the organization of the Third International, all were different and show a dialectical progression. Lenin never conceived of a mass party of two and a half million people *before* the struggle for power.

The whole of the Stalinist theory and practice of the organization of the party is based upon the administrative-bureaucratic Plan.

Conversely, the revolutionary party expands and develops its own theory on the basis of the *vast revolutionary upheavals which are stimulated in the proletariat by the structure of state-capitalism.* The European proletariat in Italy, in France, in Spain, and the American proletariat, have already shown us that from the beginning of the social revolution, the proletariat *as a whole* will be organized to become the state and to manage production. Here concretely is the embodiment of Lenin's reiterated phrase "to a man" which was impossible of realization in backward Russia in 1917.

Not only does the revolutionary proletariat of our age make its tremendous mass mobilizations. The petty-bourgeoisie does the same as in the Nazi party and the almost overnight creation of the French Rally of millions by de Gaulle. The Stalinist leaders aim to control the mass proletarian mobilizations in exactly the same manner as de Gaulle aims to control those of the petty-bourgeoisie. The Leninist party in 1950, in practice where it can, but in theory always, must be the expression of the mass proletarian mobilization aimed against the bureaucracy as such. This bureaucracy in Russia, in France and Italy (even where it is in opposition) and in the United States is the embodiment of the Plan of state-capitalism.

No question is more important theoretically, not only internally but externally, than this of the relation between party, the state and the Plan. For theoreticians and millions of workers everywhere it is the central question. No substantial section of any society today will die in defense of private property. *That* today is dead. The question is: can the nationalized property be planned without having as the inevitable consequence the domination of a single party? The popular formulation, one-party state, is absolutely and exactly right. "Johnson-Forest" have given here the essentials of the answer.

(c) What does the Fourth International have to say on this question? It can be summed up in the following: The Stalinists are criminals, opposed to democracy in the party; the Trotskyists are believers in democracy as practiced by Lenin.

The history of Trotskyist *theory* of the party, however, reinforces Stalinism in spite of all its criticism. In 1931 Trotsky believed that "with the weakening of the party or with its degeneration even an unavoidable crisis in economy can become the cause for the fall of the dictatorship." What actually took place was the reverse. When the bureaucratic-administrative Plan of the ruling class was finally substituted for the planning of the revolutionary proletariat, it was the Bolshevik party that was liquidated. State-property remained.

(d) Fifteen years later with the Bolshevik party destroyed, the Fourth International improves upon the original thesis. The World Congress thesis says: "The political dictatorship today as twenty years ago is decisive in preventing the complete collapse of planning, the breakthrough of the petty-capitalist market, and the penetration of foreign capital into Russia."

"The political dictatorship" is an abstraction. Concretely it is the party of Stalin, the murderers of the Bolshevik Party, the antithesis in every respect of the Bolshevik Party. The theory is false whether it is standing on its head or its feet, and in either form it is useless as a theoretical weapon against Stalinism.

(e) Unfortunately, this conception is not confined to Russia. The first sentence of the *Transitional Program* states that the crisis of the revolution is the crisis of revolutionary leadership. This is the reiterated theme.

Exactly the opposite is the case. It is the crisis of the self-mobilization of the proletariat. As we shall show, and it is perfectly obvious logically, this theme of orthodox Trotskyism implies that there is a competition for leadership, and that whereas the other Internationals have betrayed, the Fourth International will be honest. Exactly the contrary must be the analysis.

The concept that the whole problem is a problem of revolutionary leadership does not, cannot, upon its political premises, pose on the one hand the Stalinist leadership as clear-sighted, determined leaders with their own theory, program, policy for the enslavement of the proletariat; and opposed to them, ourselves as leaders, not simply "honest" but with a totally different conception of the role, movement and function of the proletariat. Honesty and dishonesty, sincerity and betrayal imply that we shall do what they, because of "supple spines," have failed to do. We do not propose to do what they have failed to do. We are different from them in morals because we are different from them in everything, origin, aims, purposes, strategy, tactics and ends. This fundamental antagonism "Johnson-Forest" derive from the theory of state-capitalism.

From the Stalinists' observation of state-capitalism, *their* conception of the party becomes the essence of bureaucracy, bureaucratic administration, bureaucratic organization, the bureaucratic party. For the Fourth International, on the other hand, it is a matter of life and death, in the analysis of modern economy, to counterpose what has been created by the modern economy, the mass mobilization of the proletariat and sections of the petty-bourgeoisie, as an opposition in form and content to Stalinism and the Social Democracy, and our role as a party in relation to this. To say that all the proletariat needs is revolutionary leadership drowns all differences between us and strengthens *their* conception of the party.

Trotsky at any rate was practiced in the leadership of revolution. The *Transitional Program* and particularly the conversations preceding it are sufficient indication of his profound comprehension of the mass movement. But as this whole document has shown, he gave it no theoretical basis. He did not relate it to the new stage of world economy. The result is the increased revolutionism of the masses becomes nothing else in the minds of his followers but an increased reaction to the crimes of capitalism, a mass base for leadership.

The theory as stated has had funereal consequences in our movement. Germain, for example, writes in an exhaustive analysis of the Stalinist parties: "But despite all that has been revealed about the crimes of the GPU, the large mass of Stalinist workers will continue to follow their Stalinist leaders—or will fall back into complete passivity—until the day when the Trotskyist parties can prove to them *in practice* the superiority of their policy over the policy of Stalinism" (*Fourth International*, May 1947).

In the resolution presented to the World Congress in 1948 by our European co-thinkers, there was pointed out in detail the practical consequences for politics of this conception of the party which constantly appears in the strategy and tactics of the Fourth International, particularly in France. It is the placing of this impossible, this fantastic, responsibility upon the Trotskyist organizations as they are that in the end produces Pablo.

VII
Methodology

THE MOST COMPLETE expression of Stalinist VA theory (and of any theory) is its methodology. Methodology is the result of the complex interaction of social base, theoretical analysis and practical activity, and the struggles with rival forces and rival methodologies. As it matures, it is transformed from effect into cause and in the end it is inseparable from the activity, practical and theoretical, of those who develop it.

Stalinism and Leninism

(a) The methodology of Stalinism is a methodology foretold by Marx, a combination of uncritical positivism and uncritical idealism. Its roots in bourgeois philosophy we shall take up later. The uncritical positivism is its gross materialism, its quantitative theory and practice of accumulation; its uncritical idealism is its theory of the role of intellectuals, the Plan and the party.

For such a theory, serious theoretical analysis of social phenomena is impossible. It knows no other way of achieving its aims than the method of the decadent bourgeoisie, empiricism and violence. Its theory, from the theory of ineffective demand to its analysis of the Negro question in the United States, every move in Russia, is the result and expression of empiricism and then a search in the closet of Marxism for something that will fit. If nothing is found, a new garment is created, and the Marxist label attached.

Its most glaring failure is the analysis of its own and rival movements. The analysis is entirely subjective. Stalinism inherits from Lenin the theory that the Second International was the international based upon super-profits of monopoly capitalism. There for Stalinism analysis ceases. The Stalinists, in harmony with their whole analysis of Russian social relations, are simply the most honest, the most devoted, the most

49

intelligent, enemies of capitalism and lovers of socialism. Leaders are sincere or they betray, due to malice, error, ill-intention, cowardice, bribery or corruption. Workers understand or they do not understand. As a rule, they do not understand, being corrupted by capitalist decay and the plots and deceptive propaganda of the bourgeoisie.

Every crime of Stalinism against Leninism, Popular Front, the Wallace movement, the refusal to orient toward the seizure of proletarian power—all have the one ideological base, the theory that the workers are incapable of understanding or acting. This is not mere hypocrisy. The Stalinist method is in origin and results truly capitalist, in the last stage of capitalism. In Russia and outside it is the same. Moscow trials, vilification of political opponents as thieves, *agents provocateurs*, etc., are part of the system. Stalinism aims at the subordination of the mass, its demoralization and confusion, the destruction of its capacity to think, its conversion into a large disciplined force able to trust no one or look anywhere else but to the party. Stalinism carries on a deafening agitation for mass action on separate issues which create no organic change in the qualitative relation of labor to capital. It seeks to substitute for the workers' accumulation of their historical experiences, immediate action on every occasion through committees organized and led by the party apparatus. It seeks to place the masses as much at the disposal of the party as the proletariat is at the disposal of capital.

(b) The most striking opposition to this methodology is Leninism between 1914 and 1923. The gigantic labors of 1914–17 were aimed at finding a material base for the failure of the Social-Democracy to make any resistance to the imperialist war. Lenin began with an analysis of the *specific* stage of world capitalism, the basis of every Marxist methodology. In *Imperialism* he traced the *specific* mode of production, concentration, the role of colonies, the super-profits. These super-profits were the basis of the creation of a labor aristocracy, the *specific* labor organization of capitalism at a *specific* stage.

The very structure of imperialism was, as he endlessly repeated, a transition to something higher, a higher form. The proletariat was inherently revolutionary and its revolutionary struggle for democracy was intensified by the oppression and the organization imposed upon it by capitalism itself. *This* was the basis of the foundation of the Third International. Without this theory, he insisted, "not the slightest progress" could be made. He repudiated attributing political activity on any comprehensive scale to "malice" or "evil intention." Nor did he make speculations about consciousness. The actual movement to the seizure of power was one thing, but revolutionary consciousness and desires were the product of the stage of capitalism itself.

Leninist Methodology Today

Today, where must a Leninist methodology begin?

The Fourth International as opposed to the Third can only be the product of a new stage of capitalism which has corrupted the International based upon a previous stage. This new stage we have analyzed as state-capitalism or statification of production. Without this, the International is as helpless as Lenin's Third would have been without his analysis of monopoly capitalism.

A correct methodology does not begin in a vacuum. It seeks in the Leninist analysis contained in *Imperialism* the tendencies which indicated the future developments, in this case, state-capitalism. Lenin, as Marxists always do, drew them sharply to their conclusion. The concrete facts lagged behind the theory. But because his method was irreproachable, he foresaw that in the coming period state-monopoly capitalism would end in "vast state-capitalist trusts and syndicates," that is to say, the centralizations of capital on a world scale. We live in that epoch today.

Upon these indications and using his method we seek the differences. Thus in the resolution of our co-thinkers submitted to the World Congress in 1948, *The World Political Situation and the Fourth International*, it was stated:

> Leninism in World War I analyzed the development of international capitalist monopolies which shared the world among themselves.
>
> In 1948 the movement to the centralization of capital has reached such gigantic proportions that only vast state-capitalist trusts and syndicates on a continental and intercontinental scale (Hitler's Europe, Stalinist domination of Europe and Eastern Asia, Marshall Plan, Molotov Plan, etc.) can attempt to control it. Combinations of individual capitalists from different states, organized in cartels for world combination of separate or related industries, now are—and cannot be otherwise than—a minor part of world economy.

Leninism in World War I taught that the world was completely shared out, so that in the future only redivision was possible.

In 1948 there is no question of division or redivision of the world-market. The question is posed in terms of complete mastery of the world by one of two great powers, Russia or the United States.

Leninism in World War I taught that the export of capital has become decisive as distinguished from the export of commodities, owing to the fact that capital in a few countries had become over-ripe and needed to seek a higher rate of profit in colonial countries.

In 1948 finance capital does not export surplus capital to seek higher profit. World economy now patently suffers from a shortage of capital and an incapacity to create it in sufficient quantities to reconstruct Europe and to keep production expanding. The distinction is symbolized in the qualitative difference between the Dawes Plan and the Marshall Plan.

Capital therefore tends toward centralization on a world scale. But the tendency toward centralization on a world scale and with it, the end of the world-market and of capitalist society, can be achieved only by force, i.e., the struggle for mastery between two great masses of capital, one under the control of the United States and the other under the control of Russia.

It is here that everything begins.

The tendency is the tendency to centralization on a world scale.

The tendency to centralization on a world scale can only take place by conflict between two large masses of capital. No longer cartels and distant colonies but contiguous masses of capital must be accumulated, either directly as Hitler tried to do and Stalin is doing, or through control of the state power, as the United States aims to do in Europe.

It is this double tendency of attraction and repulsion which created the necessity of state-capitalism.

The state takes over the economy, both in preparation for resisting other economies and for allying itself to the other mass of capital to which it is attracted or forced. National capital must deal with national capital.

At the same time the falling rate of profit on a world scale creates tendencies within each individual economy, both in the bureaucratic economy and, opposed to it, in the mass movement of the proletariat which is characteristic of state-capitalism.

These are the specific conditions which produce the modern bureaucracy.

The Bodyguard of Capital

Upon this analysis our co-thinkers in Europe in their 1948 resolution wrote:

> In the epoch of World War II the labor bureaucracy has undergone a qualitative development. It is no longer the "main social support" of the bourgeoisie. Such is the bankruptcy of bourgeois society that it can continue only because the labor bureaucracy has increasingly substituted itself for the bourgeoisie in the process of production itself and in the bureaucratic administration of the capitalist state. To a degree only haltingly and quite inadequately recognized by the Fourth International before the war and today, the bureaucratic leadership of the labor movement as embodied in the Communist Parties has long recognized the bankruptcy of bourgeois society, ground between the crisis in production and the growing revolt of the proletariat, the great masses of the people and the colonial masses. The bureaucracy of the Communist Parties of Europe, even before the war, sought and still seeks a new economic and social base for the maintenance and consolidation of its power over the proletariat. It is bourgeois to the core, in its terror of the proletarian revolution, in its inability to place the solution of the economic and political problems of society in the creative power of the proletariat, and in its fear of rival imperialisms. The mass of Russian capital, the Kremlin and the Stalinist Army serve it as a base from which it hopes to administer centralized European state-capitalism. With this in view it repudiates both the bourgeois national state and bourgeois

private property. It is not in any sense social-patriotic. It collaborates with the bourgeoisie or attacks it, in peace or in war, governed entirely by its immediate perspective of centralizing European capital under the aegis of Russian capital as the first stage in the struggle for world domination. In this sense its allegiance to the Kremlin is absolute. But it is essentially a product of the bankruptcy of private property and the national state on a world scale, on the one hand, and the revolutionary pressure of the masses, on the other hand.

It was pointed out that the Second International today is far closer to the bureaucracy of the Third International than it is to classic Social-Democracy.

As a result of the war, the Second International, though by tradition unsuited for the violent character of the modern class struggle, follows in essence the same basic orientation toward centralized capital. It is distinguished from the Third International by, in general, the loss of any real basis in the revolutionary proletariat, and its timidity in the face of the native bourgeoisie. In important elements it aims at the attachment of the national economy to the power of American capital. But not only in Eastern Europe where the immediate power of Russia is overwhelming, but even in Italy under the pressure of the masses and imminent economic bankruptcy, it is ready to unite with the Communist Party, i.e., attach itself to Russian capital.

The resolution also analyzed the petty-bourgeoisie upon the basis of the analysis of *state-capitalism*:

The labor bureaucracy of the Second International was always fortified by the petty bourgeoisie. Today the enormous growth of bureaucracy in the administration of capital, in the unions with their constantly expanding functions, and above all in the government, has created a huge administrative caste without which the social and economic existence of capital on a world scale would be impossible. The process of fusion between the labor bureaucracy and this petty-bourgeois administrative caste has added a new quality to the alliance between them which characterizes the period of World War II. This force constitutes the real social agency of capitalism today. Like all phenomena, the role of this bodyguard of capital varies according to specific need, more precisely, the national stage of economic bankruptcy and the revolutionary pressure of the masses. Its economic ideas are based upon the administrative concept of "planned economy." Its chief task is the subordination or corruption and blunting of the revolutionary will of the proletariat. Its basic power rests upon its control of the labor movement in the process of production itself where it is best able to check the revolutionary proletariat and preserve bourgeois society.

This is Leninism for our epoch: objective analysis of the *specific* stage of capitalist development, objective analysis of the social basis of the counter-revolutionary International, and opposed to it, of the revolutionary International.

And Orthodox Trotskyism?

What is the methodology of orthodox Trotskyism? It is to be judged by its results. It has never recognized the necessity for an analysis of the present stage of world economy. Because it never emancipated itself from the simple repetition of the facts of Lenin's *Imperialism*, it cannot get away from seeing Stalinism as reformism. Under these circumstances there is no escape whatever from subjectivism. It can offer no explanation as to why the Stalinists behave as they do. All it can attribute Stalinist practice to is evil, malice, or ill-intentions, stupidity and ignorance, supple spines, tools of the Kremlin. When it is recognized that the Stalinists are not only that, the result is Pablo.

The subjectivity of the Trotskyist analysis of Stalinism is rooted in the unrejected premise that the Stalinists are social-patriotic collaborators with their own bourgeoisie. Its catastrophic results can be seen in the Manifesto of 1940 when Trotsky faced for a few short weeks the fact that the French Stalinists had displayed a "sudden defeatism." As long as Trotskyism believed that the Stalinists would collaborate with their bourgeoisie, it could reserve for itself the idea that there was a fundamental distinction between the two Internationals. Now that events have destroyed that belief, Trotskyism is reduced to epithets.

The Fourth International is unable in objective materialist terms to find the reasons for its own existence. If it had, its present crisis over Eastern Europe would never have arisen.

The documents of the Fourth International are there to prove this. It was founded upon the basis that the Communist International was unable to learn or be taught any more (this same idea is in the *Transitional Program*; see our quote, page 4), and that the proletariat from the experience of Germany would turn away from the Comintern and toward the Fourth International. New Internationals are not founded upon the basis of the inability of the old International to learn. This mode of reasoning led to the expectation that after defeat in Germany in 1933, the Communist International would decline. The analysis was purely subjective.

Actually, it was precisely the defeat in Germany in 1933 that strengthened Stalinism. It crystallized the conviction growing in Europe that the mass revolt of the proletariat and its control of industry in the Marxist and Leninist manner were a dream. It led to the conclusion that the model of proletariat organization had to be Stalinist, and that this was the only means whereby the capitalism of private property with its crises and Fascism could be opposed. It is this that had strengthened the elements in the labor movement and the petty-bourgeoisie to make Stalinism what it is.

But at the same time it is precisely the experiences which strengthened Stalinism which have created in the proletariat the tendencies to mass mobilization for total emancipation and the creation of a mass party which will run both industry and state. These in turn strengthen the dictatorial tendencies of Stalinism.

All this is based upon economic analysis, new stages, new social responses to state-capitalism. Otherwise you have to base your new International, this colossal conception, on the fact that the old International will not "learn." In that kind of reasoning, consciousness determines existence, the existence of an organization which is to lead the greatest overturn history knows.

The inability to analyze Stalinism in the light of Leninist analysis of the present stage of capitalism cripples orthodox Trotskyism at every turn. Its analysis leans heavily on the concept of Bonapartism. The concept not only illuminates nothing, it obscures the specific stage and disguises the definitive class antagonism. The Bonapartes did not know state-capitalism, the total plan, the modern *mass parties*. The plan, the party, the state are totally capitalistic. Nazi or Stalinist, they represent capital. The great modern mass parties are either instruments of capital or instruments of the proletarian revolution. There is not the slightest element of Bonapartism in them.

Orthodox Trotskyism can find no objective necessity for an imperialist war between Stalinist Russia and American imperialism. It is the only political tendency in the world which cannot recognize that the conflict is a struggle between two powers for world mastery. It is therefore reduced to substituting subjective agitation against warmongers and profiteers, on the one hand, and attacks on Stalin for deals with imperialism, on the other.

Orthodox Trotskyism is unable because of its conception of state-property and its subjective analysis of the coming war to make the simplest distinction between the counter-revolutionary Third International and the revolutionary Fourth International: namely, that in war the former will be for one camp; the latter will be for the overthrow of both. The Fourth International today evades making this distinction by posing war as "an unlikely eventuality." Meanwhile, it puts forward both contradictory positions, alternately or simultaneously.

The Economism of Orthodox Trotskyism

Orthodox Trotskyism can merely call for a revolution in Russia. Its theory affords no objective basis for it, none. It aimed to dig a gulf between the proletariat and the bureaucracy, analyzing the proletariat alone as organically attached to state-property. With the defense of state-property by the bureaucracy, the basic Trotskyist distinction is lost.

Orthodox Trotskyism finds some base for a Russian Revolution in the "socialist consciousness" of the workers, i.e., the memories of the October Revolution. This is totally false. The socialist consciousness of the proletariat is reinforced by the October Revolution, but it is based upon the growing revolt and the unity, organization, and discipline which is the product of Russian production. So far is objective analysis lost that the impetus for the revolution of the Russian proletariat is now handed over *entirely* to agencies outside: "A new revolutionary selection, carried by a new mass upsurge, which can only be the result of a powerful revolutionary wave outside of Russia, will alone be able to restore to the proletariat a clear consciousness of its historic mission" (*Fourth International*, June 1948, 113).

This is true only if you base your analysis upon consumption.

The Russian proletariat will have to overthrow the most powerful army, state and secret police the world has ever known, to take control of production. This orthodox Trotskyism calls a political revolution, and tries to teach the workers in other countries that they have a greater task before them.

The error is as old as the opposition to Leninism. It is economism. The economists of World War I refused to support the revolt of oppressed nations because this would destroy centralization of economic forces which was progressive. Lenin fought them tooth and nail as he had fought the economists of Russia two decades before. Revolutionary struggles *produced* by a world-wide stage of economic development cannot destroy that development. Orthodox Trotskyism has never ceased to see in the kulaks, in the destruction of the party, in primitive accumulation, in war, in the restoration of religion, the source of a return to private property in Russia. This is economism at its extreme. Private property has not been restored because the whole tendency of *world economy* is in exactly the opposite direction. The strength of state-property is in the increased centralization and the vastly increased and socialized proletariat. To pose the attack on the bureaucracy by the proletariat in wartime as endangering state-property and national independence is to attribute to the bureaucracy a responsibility for state-property and Russian independence greater than that of the proletariat. It is to say that even the revolutionary proletariat of Russia is incapable, without the bureaucracy, of defending Russia and preserving state-property. On this reasoning the October Revolution would never have taken place.

Orthodox Trotskyism and the Colonial Revolts

Our final example of the inability of the Trotskyist methodology which refuses to recognize state-capitalism is the present plight of Trotskyism on the specific theory of the permanent revolution itself in relation to the colonies.

The specific theory of the permanent revolution in relation to the colonies was based on:

1. Monopoly capital exporting surplus capital to the colonial countries and industrializing them, the stage of capitalism analyzed by Lenin.

2. In this relation the native bourgeoisie would play a comprador role, collaborating with the imperialist powers.

3. The class struggle of the proletariat against the bourgeoisie and the foreign capitalists in the industrialized areas would give it the role of leader in the national struggle. The proletariat would lead the peasantry in the agrarian revolution and thereby split the petty-bourgeoisie from collaboration with the native bourgeoisie and foreign monopoly capital.

However, since the depression of 1929 and the emergence of state-capitalism on a world scale:

1. The struggle is not for redivision of colonies but for world mastery. World capitalism lives not by export of capital but by its centralization.

   (a) In the struggle for world mastery by large masses of centralized capitals, advanced countries formerly exporting capital to the colonies (France, England, Holland) are reduced to satellites of American capitalism, living on the Marshall Plan and desperate efforts to increase capital by import and further exploitation of the proletariat at home.

   (b) State loans made to the regimes of colonial countries are not used for the purpose of industrialization but for the maintenance of military outposts of the world struggle.

2. Under these conditions the continued destruction of the old feudal and handicraft economy in the countryside, going on for nearly a century, is not supplanted by any development of the industrial economy. The result is that the peasant revolts become a continuous phenomenon (uninterruptedly in China for over twenty years).

Under these changed conditions, the theory of orthodox Trotskyism about China that the peasant revolts were merely remnants of proletarian struggle and would arise only after new stimulation from the proletariat, has been outmoded by the new stage of world capitalism. These revolts, plus the world imperialist struggle, transform the national governments of the feudal landlords and native bourgeoisie, even with military support by American capitalism, into anachronisms with no perspective of national rule.

3. The new situation radicalized the urban petty-bourgeoisie. Instead of collaborating with the bankrupt bourgeoisie and remnants of foreign monopoly capital, many elements hostile to private property leave the cities to lead and control the peasant revolts. In fact, they become colonial representatives of Russian centralized capital, cadres of the Stalinist parties with relations to the revolting masses and to the power of Russia similar to those of the European Stalinists, modified but not essentially altered by their historical conditions.

4. Where, as in China, the urban petty-bourgeoisie comes to power at the head of the peasant revolt, it achieves the national independence, within the context of the international power of Stalinist Russia. Within this context, it will seek to:

    (a) expropriate the private property of the national bourgeoisie and foreign capital;

    (b) develop cadres of the petty-bourgeoisie to administer the one-party bureaucratic-administrative state of the Plan;

    (c) carry out thereby the intensified exploitation of the proletariat in production;

    (d) solve not one single problem of the agrarian revolution, which requires a complete reorganization of the economy on an international socialist basis.

In India, not the petty-bourgeoisie but Indian capital has been able to take advantage of the changed world conditions, and achieve the national independence. It is threatened by the Stalinist party which seeks to duplicate the triumph in China. The bankruptcy of the national economy lends strength to the Stalinists.

Such, in summary outline, is the analysis. Conflicts will arise, the Stalinists in the colonies may succeed or fail, completely or partially. Such is the new theoretical orientation required. Orthodox Trotskyism, on this fundamental question of its own past, here as elsewhere, is unable to solve one of the problems raised. It cannot analyze the new stage in world economy where centralization is so powerful that it achieves national independence in the colonies, using one class if another is not ready but thereby multiplying *all* the antagonisms and social crises.

VIII
Leninism and the Traditional Regime

THERE REMAINS NOW the summation of our theory—what we consider to be Leninism for our epoch. It is best explained in terms of Leninism itself in its own epoch. It is the only experience we have of the party, the plan, the state in action.

During the revolution Lenin stated that the proof that Russia was ripe for Socialism was in the creation of Soviets by the proletariat, the creation of an historic organization for the expression of its creative energies. *If the Soviets had not been created, Lenin would have held to his old doctrine of the bourgeois revolution.*

Lenin complained in the first years of the revolution that the workers were not administering the state.

Lenin complained that the state was bureaucratically deformed and called upon the party to assist the working class to be able to defend itself against its own state.

Lenin at a certain stage in the Russian Revolution stated that the party was not controlling the state and the state was running away with them and he didn't know where this monstrosity was going. Today we know or ought to.

He warned the country and the party that the few Communists in Russia were lost amid the vast number of bourgeois functionaries of the old regime.

Lenin recognized the need for individual management in the sense of petty-bourgeois functionaries and subordination in industry to a single will. But he drew a harsh line between the proletariat and the Bolshevik Party, on the one hand, and those whom the Stalinists and Titoists call the "socialist intelligentsia."

61

In *Left Wing Communism* he pointed out that absolutely the most difficult task of all tasks for the proletariat and its party was the conversion of the petty-bourgeois intelligentsia into loyal and disciplined servants of *the proletariat state*. The petty-bourgeoisie, to whose individualism Lenin referred in 1920 as being in direct opposition to the aims and methods of the proletariat, is today infinitely more dangerous. The petty-bourgeois has transferred his individualism into "collectivism" which he understands to be statified production, administration and plan, and is now the firm ally of the labor bureaucracy of capital, the plan, *against* the revolutionary proletariat.

The essence of Leninism may be summed up as follows:

1. The state was necessary for the destruction of the exploiters. But this state was a danger to the proletariat. It was the task of the party to protect the proletariat against the state and "to utilize state measures for the purpose of protecting the material and spiritual interests of the entirely organized proletariat from the state."

2. The backwardness of the Russian economy and the predominance of the peasantry imposed upon Russian production the necessity for the leadership of technicians, bureaucrats, planners, etc. But in the same way that the proletariat had to be protected against its own state, the proletariat had also to be protected against the necessary bureaucracy. This was the beginning and end of Leninist policy. You understand nothing about the Russian Revolution and the problems of the proletariat, the party and the state, unless you understand this.

These were the problems that could be resolved only by merging them into the world and particularly the European socialist revolution.

Lenin always sought for initiative. It was initiative which he sought in 1921 by the NEP, and to the very last, in his insistence on the significance of cooperatives.

The following quotation exemplifies how he proposed to struggle against the dangers that threatened the Soviet order:

> We possess profound sources of strength, a broad and deep reservoir of human material, such as is not possessed, and never will be possessed, by any bourgeois government. We

have material upon which we can draw ever more deeply, by passing from the advanced workers, not only to the average workers, but even lower to the toiling peasants, to the poor and poorest peasants. Comrades from Petrograd were recently saying that Petrograd has given all its political workers and cannot give more. But when the critical hour struck, Petrograd, as Comrade Zinoviev justly remarked, proved magnificent, it seemed to be a city which was giving birth to new forces. Workers who appeared to be below the average level, who had no state or political experience whatsoever, rose to their full height and provided numerous forces for propaganda, agitation and organization, and performed miracle after miracle. Our source of miracles is still very great.

This is the Leninist policy, the basic policy which applies to every question of transitional regime. The concrete circumstances will differ, but the *less powerful the situation of the proletariat, the more necessary, particularly after thirty years, becomes the Leninist policy.* That is the decisive test and not abstract arguments about whether the country is ready for socialism.

The application of this Leninist policy is not a question for the future, *after* the difficulties of the transitional regime have been solved. It is the first step of revolutionary policy, from the very beginning, from the moment of the conquest of power. This was Lenin's conception of the transitional regime, and this is what Trotsky, quoting Lenin on the struggle against officialdom, described as Lenin's policy: "You must not think that Lenin was talking about the problems of a decade. No, this was the first step with which 'we should and must begin upon achieving a proletarian revolution'" (*The Revolution Betrayed*, 50, emphasis in original).

This also is the reason for Lenin's emphasis on the world proletariat. To anybody who saw the proletariat as Lenin did in relation to its own proletarian state and its own bureaucracy, the revolution of the proletariat in the advanced countries was an imperative necessity. The idea that the Yugoslav leaders are going to learn from books that the world revolution is necessary, which they didn't know before, illuminates what orthodox Trotskyism thinks of the theory of socialism in a single country. If the Yugoslav leaders saw the proletariat with the eyes of those trying to lead the workers' state in relation to the rest of the population, not books but the necessity of preserving the workers' state would have driven them to the world revolution long before the break with Stalin.

The Leninist policy is dialectical to the core. It is based upon a brutal recognition of the contradictions within the workers' state. It is permeated with the spirit of the revolutionary proletariat: the revolutionary mobilization of the masses against the bourgeoisie in the first stage. Then when the workers' state had been established, to protect against the inevitable encroachments and invasions by its own state, the independence and creative initiative of the proletariat which had begun by creating the Soviets.

Lenin's mastery of dialectic, his conviction that socialism could be created only by an emancipated proletariat, enabled him to discover the contradiction and outline revolutionary policy when the majority of his colleagues, it is clear, had no conception that such a contradiction could exist. Today there is no excuse. The maturity of state-capitalism has brought the contradiction which Lenin sensed into the open. This dominates our epoch. Without the Leninist conception, thoroughly mastered, you end in active uncritical support of the bureaucratic-administrative one-party state. The proof is Yugoslavia.

IX
Yugoslavia

We have to remind orthodox Trotskyism that it did not support the *European movement* for national liberation when the masses were in motion. Now it proposes to support the *national state* of Yugoslavia in the struggle for national independence against the Kremlin. This is the state which suppressed the mass movement, subordinated it to the movements of the Russian Army and kept it from making contact with the European mass movement. The policy stands on its head.

In reality it is the criterion of state-property which explains this consistently false policy. Unless it is a question of nationalized property vs. private property, orthodox Trotskyism cannot see and interpret the movement of the proletariat. The moment nationalized property is involved, it starts looking for the mass pressures and actions to explain this nationalization.

Compare with this the policy of "Johnson-Forest." Whereas in 1943 the Shachtmanites plunged headlong into the liberation movement under the slogans of struggle for democracy and national independence, "Johnson-Forest" took the position that the proletariat and the party should enter the national liberation movement and struggle for proletarian power under the general slogan of the Socialist United States of Europe.[1] Thus, right from the beginning, we posed the struggle inside the Yugoslav movement against the national policy of Titoism. That is still the basis of our position today.

For orthodox Trotskyism, on the other hand, then as now, the Socialist United States of Europe remains an abstraction. The International

---

1   Resolution on the National and Colonial Struggle for Freedom, July 20th, 1943. Published in part in the *New International* (December 1943) as "The National Question and the European Socialist Revolution." See also "The Way Out for Europe," *New International* 9, nos. 4–5 (April–May 1943): 116–19.

is now busily debating when the revolution took place in Yugoslavia. Characteristically, it does not occur to the debaters to ask themselves how this highly exceptional, extremely silent revolution took place unnoticed by the leaders of the revolutionary movement. That would be bad enough. But in 1945 or 1946 or 1947 (etc., etc.) this revolution presumably took place unnoticed by the proletariat in the surrounding countries of Europe and the rest of the world.

However, what concerns us now is the situation in Yugoslavia.

Extensive documents have been published by the Communist Party of Yugoslavia (CPY) itself. "Johnson-Forest" do not for one single moment take these documents as true representations of the history of Yugoslavia for the last ten years. As well accept the documents of Stalinist bureaucrats as the history of Russia. But they are the basis of the politics and discussion of all tendencies in the Fourth International today. We accept them therefore to the degree that in themselves, they represent, if not the history of Yugoslavia on the whole, a clear representation of the theory and politics of the Yugoslav leaders.

Titoism is pure conscious consistent Stalinism. Having a model in both the theory and practice of Russia already established, Titoism has been able to achieve in a few short years the counter-revolutionary climax which it took Stalin nearly two decades to accomplish. Stalin had to struggle against the traditions and remnants not of capitalism but of Leninism. Tito *began* as a finished Stalinist.

The Trade Unions in Yugoslavia

Stalinism in Russia provided the CPY with the model for disciplining the workers by transforming the trade unions from organs of struggle by the workers into organs of mobilization of the workers to speed up production. The CPY explains why it destroyed the trade unions as militant class organizations of the working class:

> Under the conditions in the new Yugoslavia, after the na-
> tionalization of industry, and as a result of the quick tempo
> of socialist building, the workers' class is no longer a class
> of bare-handed proletarians which must fight a daily po-
> litical and economic struggle, which must fight for more

bread. This class today—in alliance with the other working masses—holds the authority—holds the greater part of the means of production, and its future depends in the first place on itself, on its work, and on its unity with other toilers, on the mobilization of all toilers in socialist building.

This is the exact opposite of Leninism. It is pure Stalinism. The independence of the working class, its struggles to protect its material and spiritual interests, its leadership of the other working masses, its determination of policy—all these are the mortal enemy of the one-party bureaucratic administrative state and in the sacred name of nationalized property, all these are to be destroyed.

To achieve this statification of the trade unions, the CPY "liquidated the old guild-like dispersion of the union organizations, united manual and intellectual workers into one organization, and mobilized them in the building of the country, in the building of socialism."

This unity of manual and intellectual workers is a sure sign of the Labor Front of the "corporate state." It is a means of subordinating the workers to the petty-bourgeois intellectuals and administrators. Management spies, Stakhanovites, time-study men—the whole apparatus of supervision and domination is brought into the trade unions. They become the representatives of the state inside the unions. The trade unions then have the task to "develop the new relationship of the working class and the working masses in general toward work . . . organize socialist competition and shockwork, rationalization and innovation . . . fight for work discipline, to improve the quality of work, to guard the people's property, to struggle against damage, against absenteeism, against careless work and similar things."

While carrying on these disciplinary functions the trade unions are "to explain to the working masses that such a struggle is in their own interests, in the interest of the working masses in general." Cripps and Attlee, in capitalist Britain, would consider three-fourths of their troubles solved if they could instruct the British labor unions, suitably poisoned with "socialist intelligentsia," to carry out the economic plans of the state. Tito, the Stalinist in the one-party bureaucratic administrative state, considers that it is his right to instruct the trade unions accordingly, and all because the property is state-owned.

The Titoists leave the workers in no uncertainty as to what all this means. It is resistance to speed-up which is involved. "It is necessary to point out that in many trade union organizations there are still many remnants of social-democratic conceptions and opportunism which is manifested on the one hand in resistance to fulfillment of the plan and in resistance to realistic norms, to competition, and on the other hand in exaggerated demands in regard to pay."

To these miserable elements no mercy will be shown. As in Stalinist Russia, the basis has been laid for war to the end against them by placing them in the realm of social-democratic, i.e., *capitalist* ideology, in opposition to socialist building. *They* are the enemy.

The organizers of increased production, on the other hand, are the cadres. These have caught on quickly because as the whole history of industry shows, that is not hard to learn. In fact (this was written by Kardelj in 1948), they had too "correctly grasped the organizing role of the trade unions in production." "In practice, in carrying out the economic-organizational tasks of the trade unions, our trade union cadres often go to extremes." They "forgot" certain "other equally important tasks." And what did they forget? They simply forgot "concern for the welfare of the workers, struggle for better living conditions for them and work on the political elevation of the working masses."

And why is such forgetfulness harmful and why must it be corrected? Is it because only by this means will a new economy superior to capitalism be developed? Not at all. It is because not to be concerned about these things would weaken the respect of the proletariat for the state authority.

The trade unions are the "direct organizers of the struggle of the working class for the increase in production." But "the workers must feel that their trade union organization is concerned with their welfare." Imagine the denunciations that would fall from orthodox Trotskyism on the head of Reuther if he dared to say, as indeed he would not at this stage, that it is the business of Reutherite cadres to make the workers "feel" that the union is concerned with their welfare and working conditions. But transfer private property into state-property, and forthwith this becomes "proletarian policy." This is Stalinism and nothing else but Stalinism.

Lenin insisted on the need for the proletariat to protect itself against its own state. The CPY labels resistance by the proletariat to fulfillment of the plan as "incorrect," "unfriendly," "backward." This is typical Stalinist phraseology and in Russia is accompanied by keeping millions in the forced labor camps where these backward elements are "reeducated." The Titoists ask for "healthy criticism by the working masses through the mass organizations as regards the work of the state organs, economic and social institutions, etc." The phrasing is accurate and well-chosen. Individual workers and groups of workers must not complain. They can only criticize through the mass organizations, i.e., through the trade union cadres. Resistance to speed-up, for example, leads to the conclusion that one "does not want to see where the real interests of the working class lie." It is obvious that criticism by such a worker would be unhealthy, unhealthy for the state and no doubt unhealthy for this "irresolute," "unfriendly" and "backward" worker.

The Mode of Labor in Yugoslavia

Competition is the Titoist method for intensifying the speed of production. Again Stakhanovism in Stalinist Russia provided the model for the CPY.

On New Year's Eve in 1947 Marshall Tito boasted that "this spirit of competition has begun to penetrate into our state administration and other institutions as well." The bureaucracy introduced its own special type of incentive pay. By great activity in speed-up and shockwork, a worker could get out of the proletariat altogether and join the bureaucracy. As the Titoists explain: "Factory and workshop department heads, and often directors of factories and enterprises are being culled from the ranks of shockworkers."

The factory directors selected in this manner provided the nucleus for the stratification in production, formalized in the New Five-Year Plan of 1947. Again the administrative plan of Stalinist Russia provided the model. The CPY consciously organizes production according to the principle of the hierarchy in production which, as we have explained, Marx analyzed as the heart of capitalist authority. In introducing the Five-Year Plan it writes: "Planned economy of itself imposes the need of a planned distribution of labor-power, the planned training and development of technical cadres."

The creation of "our people's, our socialist intelligentsia," which Stalin had to wait until the 1936 Constitution to systematize, is organized by Tito after a few years of power.

Article 14 of the New Five-Year Plan of 1947 is entitled "Work and Cadres." It reads:

> 1. To ensure a steady increase in the productivity of work by introducing the greatest possible mechanization, new methods of work, new technological processes and norms of work, by improving the qualifications of the workers, and by *thoroughly utilizing working hours*" (emphasis added).

There must be no waste of time of the workers at work. The passage goes on to repeat the Stalinist theory with regard to the intensification of the rate of exploitation: "thus creating the conditions for an increase of wages and better remuneration for workers of all categories. In connection with this to perfect a system of *progressive payments for work over and above the norm, as well as a system for premia for engineering and technical staffs, for the fulfillment of the plan*" (emphasis added).

Not only the planning of incentive pay for the workers. Planning of incentive pay also to the bureaucracy in order to inspire them to intensify the exploitation of the workers.

The Plan calls for special training of an expanded administrative cadre:

> 3. to ensure the increase of the cadres with secondary professional training from 65,000 in 1946 to 150,000 in 1951, effecting this by opening new technical secondary schools and enlarging existing ones. . . .

> 4. to ensure an increase in the number of experts with university qualifications to an average of 5,000 annually. . . . To carry out a planned enrolment in all faculties and professional schools, thus providing the most important sectors with the necessary cadres.

For Yugoslavia as for Stalinist Russia, this social inequality is not a question of enjoying cultural privileges over and above those of the workers. The purpose of the Plan is to "direct all technically trained intelligentsia toward creative work," i.e., to devise new methods for the administration of the proletariat against the very conditions of large-scale production. The Titoists, having enunciated the magic phrase, state-property, think they have no such problems.

The political economy of Titoism is the political economy of Stalinism.

Stalinist theory within the last decade, for reasons that we have explained, has developed the idea that the law of value also exists in socialism. The CPY follows this faithfully, claiming that the law of value is "fully under control" because there is "state control" and "market regulation." Like the Stalinists, they claim that there is "no surplus value in the socialist sector" because there is no private appropriation of surplus labor. Then comes a remarkable sentence. We are told: "Surplus labor has the odd property that it can be materialized in new instruments of labor which make for greater productivity in labor: hence a spiral tendency."

The Marxist general law of capitalist accumulation consists precisely of the terrible effects upon the proletariat and ultimately upon production of this very "spiral tendency" of "surplus labor." The "oddity" of this surplus labor under capitalism, as distinguished from previous societies, is precisely its materialization into instruments of labor which dominate over the proletariat. Kidric's description of the process as "odd" merely highlights the obvious. The main aim of the bureaucracy is identical with that of the bourgeoisie under private property capitalism: the acceleration of this spiral tendency of materializing surplus labor into new instruments of labor for the intensification of the rate of exploitation.

At the same time Kidric knows from his Russian model that "socialist accumulation" consists not only of exploitation, but also of the state "sharing" the workers' wages through taxation. Kidric states that "so long as there is surplus labor on the one hand . . . and forces of production on the other which are not so developed as to make it possible to raise the standard of living as we should like to, to build new factories, implements of labor, etc., to the extent and in the place where we should like to, there exists a possibility of incorrect usage, a possibility of incorrect distribution of surplus labor."

This is not mere talk about economic theory. It is the justification for adding to the exploitation of the workers in the process of production, the most merciless method of taxation the modern world has known. In the *New International* of December 1942 and January–February 1943, Forest has made a study of the turnover tax in Stalinist Russia and has shown how this tax, levied chiefly on consumption goods of the poor, supplied 60% to 75% of the national budget. The tax was graduated, the highest tax was on bread, leading to a tenfold increase in the sale price. One of the lowest taxes in the consumption goods field was on silk, and it was a mere one percent on means of production goods. It is upon this model that there was fastened upon the Yugoslav people in 1947 the turnover tax on goods, a "typically socialist form of socialist monetary accumulation tried out in practice in the Soviet Union." As a result of this turnover tax, "state accumulation has grown in 1947 to 276% as compared with 1946."

Speed-up in production, planned organization of cadres to utilize thoroughly the working hours of the proletariat, accumulation of surplus value, domination of new instruments of labor over the proletariat—this is the mode of production in Yugoslavia; and from this is inseparable the one-party administrative state and the party of the bureaucracy.

The One-Party Bureaucratic-Administrative State of the Plan

The Yugoslav Communist Party leaders have known from the beginning that they have one "basic problem—the problem of authority."

After the invasion of German Fascism, there never was such an opportunity in the world so far in which to establish a genuine Soviet state. But the CPY, faced with the destruction of the old bourgeois state and seeing further that it would face the revolutionary proletariat and the revolutionary masses, from the very beginning set out to establish the most powerful bourgeois state that it could. It established "a unified state authority"—"from top to bottom . . . firmly linked into one unified system on the basis of vertical ties between the various branches of state authority and administration and the lower organs, whose duty it is within the framework of the competence of the higher organs to carry out all the tasks which they put before them."

This which Lenin feared is what the CPY sought. They were plotting this as far back as 1943. Over and over again they boast that they were the first of the Eastern European countries to achieve the formation of the state apparatus.

Marx on the Commune and Lenin in every page of his writings on the Russian Revolution saw as the first task of the revolution the mobilization of the masses as the beginning of the *destruction* of all state authority. The strong centralized state was necessary only against the exploiters and against the enemy abroad. But in Yugoslavia the exploiters had been destroyed as never before. Yugoslavia was surrounded by friendly states and enjoyed the powerful protection of the Red Army. The powerful state authority was therefore directed *against the mass movement* and could have been directed against nothing else. It is not only that this state authority expressed the instinctive self-defense of the petty-bourgeoisie against the revolutionary proletariat, a lesson which Marxism has spent so many thousands of pages trying to teach. It is that the Titoists had a model. They knew what they wanted. They are Stalinists.

They modeled and still model themselves on the one-party state, the bureaucratic plan and the party of Stalin. They insist on the differences between the development of Yugoslavia and the Russian *Revolution.* But they give credit where credit is due and say that they have been "governed by the rich experiences from the development and work of the authorities of the USSR." Let orthodox Trotskyism explain this.

Any *workers' state*, particularly in a small peasant country, in sheer self-defense has to establish the independence of the proletariat as the first safeguard of the proletarian revolution and of the proletarian character of the party. Leninism established this by weighting the vote of the proletariat 5 to 1 against the vote of the peasantry. Titoism sought from the outset to dissolve the class independence of the workers in a People's Front. The Titoists tell us themselves how they sought to strengthen "the alliance of the working class with the working peasantry, the people's intelligentsia and other toilers, and with all patriotic forces within the country, an alliance which was given organizational form in the People's Front."

Note now the characteristically Stalinist method of analysis which we have earlier explained as based upon the necessity to disguise the class nature of the bureaucracy and the state. The Titoists say that the only people excluded were "anti-people's elements," the category in which Stalinism has always lumped all those who disagreed with its policies. Coalition with political parties played no significant role in this People's Front because with the destruction of the old national bourgeois state apparatus, the objective framework of the old political parties had been destroyed. This facilitated the Titoist aim of extending the mass base of the movement beyond the working class. Bourgeois and petty-bourgeois elements could enter into the People's Front on an equal basis, unidentified with their old political banners.

To destroy the class independence of the workers was to facilitate the control and authority over the workers by the party. The CPY boasts that "there was no other force outside the CPY which could unite the peoples of Yugoslavia and the working masses." The Titoists fought "determinedly against too sudden changes which might have narrowed the mass base of the National Liberation uprising." "The basic thing in the People's Front is that it is a broad form of political organization." This "eases the realization of the leading role of the Party."

From this broad base the party could recruit the most active, militant and devoted fighters, regardless of class affiliation, to form the cadre and the executive apparatus of the state for the next stage of the counter-revolution. Once the objective basis for class differentiation is buried in the united mass movement, the only basis for differentiation of policy is subjective and opportunistic, behind which loyalty to the party and the bureaucratic apparatus can be disguised as devotion to the proletarian revolution. The type of "initiative," "activity," "devotion," "efficiency," "loyalty" required is that which enables the petty-bourgeoisie to rise to the top and administer the rest of the population. Instead of the working class and its vanguard leading the masses, the party cadres selected from the all-inclusive mass movement rule the working class. The party becomes the apparatus for the one-party bureaucratic-administrative state.

During the trade union discussion and afterwards, Lenin directed the most violent internal polemic of the whole October Revolution against the bureaucracy and the militarism which had grown up as a result of the need for mobilizing the whole country as a war machine. This played a great role in the destruction of proletarian power in the Russian Revolution. Precisely these war experiences had obviously assisted the CPY in its frantic attempt to establish the state and the centralized power.

The Titoists themselves boast that with the end of the war "the new authority then already had a firm skeleton, the new state apparatus, grown and tried in the fires of war, with new tested cadres which had already attained quite a wealth of experience during the war from the work of the people's authorities on the liberated territory." This powerful state was the means whereby they would rule the economy.

If we want a demonstration of Lenin's thesis that even confiscation without the power of the proletariat means tyranny for the proletariat, we have an example in Yugoslavia. The statification of production was carried out from beginning to end by the bureaucratic-administrative one-party state. Even before the final defeat of Nazi Germany, the property of the collaborators was confiscated by the "unified people's authority" at the III Session of the Anti-Fascist Council of the National Liberation of Yugoslavia in 1944. The steady strengthening of the state apparatus made it possible to complete nationalization formally in December 1946, by the same means. The workers remained at their benches. The Titoists announce this triumphantly: "Nationalization was well prepared organizationally and was carried out in such a way that sabotage and damage were made impossible. All enterprises in the entire country were taken over on the same day and almost at the same time *without the stopping of production*" (emphasis added).

The Titoists first suppressed the mass movement and then liquidated the bourgeoisie.

Following their model, Stalinism, in theory and in practice, the Titoists declare that this nationalization is socialism. They say: "The confiscation of property . . . possessed in essence the character of a socialist measure. Why? Firstly, because it was carried out by the people's authority as the authority of the revolutionary working people headed by the working class. Secondly, because confiscated property passed into the hands of the people in general, into the hands of the working people's state as the manager of this property, and therefore it was clear from the outset that it would crystallize into property of a purely socialist type." Note here the careful substitution of the people in general for the revolutionary workers and the immediate substitution of the state for the people in general.

As in Stalinist Russia, every measure against the workers is justified in the name of socialism, because where the working class—that is to say, the people in general; that is to say, the working people's state; that is to say, the manager of the property—owns the means of production, the workers have no interest separate and apart from those of the state, which is in reality the manager of the property, which is to say, the people in general, etc., etc.

Stalinism in a Very Single, Very Small, Very Backward Country

The Fourth International believes that when the Titoists broke with Stalin, Tito thereby began to move to the Left. We stand absolutely bewildered before this kind of Marxism. How could Tito or anyone in his situation move "to the Left"? The Titoist state was modeled upon the Russian Stalinist state. Tito had now lost his international connections. It was now Yugoslavia pursuing the identical methods of the one-party bureaucratic-administrative state of Plan in a very single, very small, very backward country, confronted by Western imperialism on the one hand, and with the hostility of the whole of Stalinist-controlled Eastern Europe facing it on the other. The theory of Trotskyism from the beginning had been that it was precisely such circumstances which had driven Stalinist Russia to degeneration. What belief in miracles is it to think that at this time, Tito, professed and practicing Stalinist, would move "to the Left"? The only policy the Titoists could follow was the strengthening of the dictatorship of the one-party, bureaucratic-administrative state of the Plan; increase in discipline over the workers in order to atone for the difficulties of isolation in the only way that the bureaucracy can; the accelerated spiral tendency of accumulation to maintain some place of some kind for Yugoslavia on the world market.

The Titoists were compelled to accelerate all tendencies they had hitherto followed. But in characteristic Stalinist fashion, they combined this with the most extravagant demagogy.[2] It is precisely the break with Stalin which has made the Titoist state more Stalinist than ever.

In 1949 a New Law on People's Committees was elaborated. Behind all the phrases on increased participation of the people, one theme

---

2 For every CPY statement about the need to struggle against bureaucracy and for democracy, it is possible to find twenty in the Stalinist documents written at precisely the moment when they were massacring revolutionists.

dominated. It was the need for "legality and discipline within the state administrative apparatus—these are the two powerful means for strengthening the state system as a whole."

"Legality and discipline"—legality for the state, discipline for the workers.

The growth of the Soviet state terrified Lenin. Kardelj's report on the New Law reaffirms the counter-revolutionary Stalinist thesis that in a socialist state "the administrative apparatus is greatly expanded and becomes more complicated." Precisely because the problem is not only regulation and control but economic management, the report repeats without equivocation the prerogatives in production of the state authority. "It is necessary to combine the administrative sectors as firmly as possible along vertical lines, not only in the sense of subordinating the lower organs to the higher, and seeing to it that the directives of the higher organs are carried out, but also in the sense of making the higher organs more helpful to the lower."

The vertical line—that is to say, domination of the people's committees by the centralized state.

The bureaucracy sought—not like Lenin for new sources of strength among the deep masses of the workers—in its crisis, it sought to strengthen the state authority by new recruitments from those who have shown readiness in the factories to exceed the norms in production.

Having now piled up bureaucracy upon bureaucracy in the very vitals of production and politics, the Titoists indulge in the characteristic Stalinist "self-criticism" of bureaucratic tendencies as rudeness, inefficiency, red-tape, etc. A report by Tito in December 1946 had already defined bureaucratism as "different incorrectnesses," among them, "The incorrect attitude toward peoples, often toward the best workers, both manual and intellectual," "incorrectnesses toward national property, squandering, etc."

Kardelj in 1949 chides the cadres for bureaucratism in the characteristic Stalinist manner. "It is necessary to declare war to the bitter end" against "a bureaucratic soulless and rude attitude toward the citizenry; absence of efforts . . . to improve the appearance of the buildings and premises of the people's committees, etc."

Against "bureaucratically minded persons" the criticism and self-criticism of the CPY is wearisomely resolute. It issues decrees for "decentralization." As long as the bureaucracy has its cadres at the core and head of every factory administration and people's committee, decentralization means the exact opposite of increased democracy and control by the workers. The ground is laid for the competition of factory against factory, as we have described it for Stalinist Russia. The Titoists issue decrees for workers' control of production. On the basis of "socialist competition," the Stalinist-Titoist mode of labor, workers' control of production is shockworkers' control of production. For the mass of workers, the perspective is intensified domination by the one-party bureaucratic-administrative state of the Plan.

The CPY, the Red Army, and the Break with the Kremlin

The Yugoslav state was formed, not because of the European revolution but because of the power of the Red Army. Backing up the CPY was the counter-revolutionary army which went through Europe, destroying the proletarian revolution, and above all, the very national liberation movement in Europe which was headed for a proletarian revolution, the Polish movement. The *Warsaw insurrectionists* were beheaded by Stalin and the Red Army. The *Yugoslav state* was formed with the assistance of Stalin and the Red Army. The Yugoslav leaders say so. They say so again and again: "The increasingly strong international role of the USSR opened a perspective to small peoples also of not only being able to liberate themselves from the imperialist chain but of being able to preserve and develop further the revolutionary achievements of the National Liberation War."

They cannot minimize the blanket of protection given by the Soviet Union: "The new historic condition in the construction of our socialist economy consists in this—in view of the great victory of the Soviet Union over German fascism and its efforts to gain world domination, and in view of the inception of the new people's democracies, made possible by the victory of the Soviet Union, our revolution could not be encircled by capitalist neighbors, to the same threatening extent as was the case of the October Revolution."

This is exactly the mentality of Stalinists all over the world. They cannot place the solution of the economic and political problems in the creative power of the proletariat. They are afraid of rival imperialisms.

They do not depend on the proletarian revolution on an international scale. They seize the power when the Red Army is at their backs.

The break with Stalin made it necessary for the CPY to find another international base to strengthen its hand against the Yugoslav proletariat. "Socialism in a single country" is only secondarily nationalist. Its class essence which it cannot abandon is bureaucratic domination over the proletariat. In this epoch all states must combine defense of their rule over their own proletariat with an international appeal to sections of the population in other countries. Yesterday Stalin combined collective security maneuvers with imperialist powers (League of Nations, Fascist Germany, Churchill) with manipulations of the parties of the Comintern. Today, Tito combines his national security deals with American imperialism, participation in the UN and expansionist designs in the neighboring countries, with the call for a new internationalism. Every manipulation of the Third International by Stalin serves one purpose, defense of the one-party state and bureaucratic-administrative Plan of the Russian centralization of capital. Tito's present maneuvers in internationalism are a model of imitation. The theory of internationalism is the same in both cases: rally whatever forces are available on an international scale to support "socialist building" in Russia or very backward Yugoslavia and identify this with the advance of the world revolution. The defense of Yugoslavia attracts particularly those seeking an escape from the stranglehold of the two great masses of capital, without the world revolutionary perspective of revolutionary class struggle against the bureaucracy in each country.

As we wrote in October 1949:

> The essence of the struggle can be seen by its effects upon the world working class movement. Whereas the labor lackeys of the Second International carefully refrained from any assistance to Ethiopia or Republican Spain, they are ready to support the bourgeoisie in stimulation of Tito's opposition to Stalin. The past and present of the Titoist party, in the present world crisis, make Tito a pole of attraction far more to the supporters of Western imperialism than to the genuinely revolutionary masses." ("No Support to Tito," *Internal Bulletin*, October 1949)

Stalinism has lived and can live only by the perpetual purging of elements in the bureaucracy, particularly those who occupy any prominence. Tito understood quite clearly that carrying out the policy of the Kremlin ends inevitably in one's own neck being in jeopardy. He knew this from his whole past association with the frame-ups and assassinations of the Kremlin, and the events in post-war Eastern Europe were bringing this home to him with a very intimate urgency.

This was the position that confronted the Titoist bureaucracy. Does any orthodox Trotskyist deny this? Objectively, the Titoist bureaucracy was caught between the Kremlin and the Yugoslav masses. The native bourgeoisie had been so thoroughly destroyed that the CPY had no buffer between it and the masses. It therefore faced this situation. Either to try to impose the Kremlin's demands upon the Yugoslav masses, which meant inevitably whether the demands were carried out or not, the sacrificing of substantial elements in the bureaucracy. (The more it imposed these demands on the Yugoslav masses, the less would it be able to use its mass base to defend itself against the inevitable purge.) Or to attempt to defy the Kremlin and lean for support on the masses in Yugoslavia and the rival imperialism, taking advantage of shifts in the world situation.

Tito was able to break with the Kremlin because he had a mass base. But precisely this situation poses the revolutionary and counter-revolutionary alternatives with extreme sharpness.

It is one thing to say that "Stalin's most pliant and devoted agents" were "forced into a struggle with the Kremlin in order to preserve their influence and leadership *over the masses*" (*Fourth International*, October 1949, emphasis added). This leaves the door open to revolutionary struggle against the Titoist bureaucracy.

It is quite another to identify the revolutionary struggles of the Yugoslav masses with Tito's attacks against the Kremlin and his break with Stalin. This opens the door to ever more uncritical support of Tito. It drives the Yugoslav masses into national unity with the CPY bureaucracy in state power, encourages illusions regarding the mythical national independence of Yugoslavia, and bars the way to the only escape from Stalinist domination, the joint revolutionary struggles of the masses in Eastern Europe and Russia, against the Stalinist bureaucracy in all its forms and for the Socialist United States of Europe.

The importance of this is not only in relation to Yugoslavia. The contradictions of Stalinism are immense, and as the world crisis develops, will appear in a multitude of forms. Titoism is only one. It is the substitution of *national unity* against foreign domination *with the bureaucracy in state power*, for class struggle *against that bureaucracy*. The danger of support to Titoism is that it presupposes and fortifies the conception that the breakup of Stalinism will come from competing elements in the bureaucracy, and particularly from the national bureaucracies in state power, rather than from the mass revolutionary struggle against the bureaucracy as such.

The proletarian revolution against Stalinism will be of necessity from its very beginnings concretely international. The *concretely* nationalist and *abstractly* internationalist orientation of Titoism, on the other hand, is not at all accidental and has its own logic. The CPY's efforts to maintain a mythical independence will land it either in the camp of Western imperialism or back in the Kremlin camp, even if to achieve this latter alternative, the bureaucratic cadre must rid itself of Tito, Kardelj, etc.

This is not abstract theory, speculation, or psychoanalysis of the CPY. In their own documents, published for all the world to see, since the split with Stalin, the Titoists themselves have proclaimed their aims, methods, and fundamental economic theories. They are Stalinist to the core: the one-party state, the bureaucratically administered plan, the export of petty-bourgeois liberalism for international consumption. Every step that they ask the world proletariat to take in their defense is for one purpose and one purpose only—to strengthen the position of the Yugoslav national capital on the world-market and the Yugoslav unified state authority over and against the Yugoslav masses. At the same time, every defense of its national capital, in the present struggle for world mastery between the two great masses of capital, only centralizes it further for attraction into one orbit when it is repelled from the other.

Such is the "Johnson-Forest" analysis of Yugoslavia. On reading *The Invading Socialist Society* some critics shrugged their shoulders and said that it had little connection with practical politics. We point out to them without malice that it is precisely from this analysis that we are able to give a strictly materialistic account of the economic, social and political development of Yugoslavia. On the other hand, the presumed practical politics of orthodox Trotskyism has resulted in this: that its whole analysis can be summed up in the question whether the leaders of the CPY are sincere or insincere in their protestations about democracy.

The Counter-Revolution in Yugoslavia

The debate now going on in the Fourth International as to when the revolution took place in Yugoslavia obviously does not involve us directly, since we do not believe that any revolution took place in Yugoslavia at all. However, to assist the debate, we would remind the comrades of the following accounts of the events in Yugoslavia. At the time these accounts were written, we accepted them, and contrary to the other tendencies in the Fourth International, still accept them.

How was the revolution in Yugoslavia crushed? At the time that the Titoist bureaucracy strangled the mass movement in Yugoslavia, everybody knew it. It was described in the *Fourth International* in careful detail. The Titoist bureaucracy was singled out as an example of a police dictatorship on the Stalinist model:

> During the War, Stalinist bureaucratization and suppression must have proceeded apace along with the growth of the popular movement and the promulgation of the social revolutionary measures. For no sooner was the present government installed than it began to emulate all the other East European police regimes in its savagery and terror. The correspondents reported that an atmosphere of fear pervaded the Capital and that the dreaded secret police, the OZNA, were operating everywhere. Tito is imitating Stalinist Russia even to copying the elegantly cut uniforms of the Kremlin bureaucrats and weighting down his military tunic with countless shining medals. The black reactionary character of Stalinism is exposed by its need of a police dictatorship in Yugoslavia—a country where it enjoyed tremendous popularity and support. This development cannot be explained solely on the grounds of the horrible economic dislocations. It was unquestionably bred by Tito's twin needs of not only suppressing the old

counter-revolutionary classes but at the same time keeping an iron hand on the working class and preventing their
emergence as an independent—nonbureaucratized—
and therefore anti-Stalinist force." (*Fourth International*,
November 1946)

It would be hard to duplicate this account for accuracy. This was in 1946
when orthodox Trotskyism considered Yugoslavia a capitalist state.

Since the break with the Kremlin, the writer has evolved the position that Yugoslavia is a workers' state, but he has not lost his eye for
accurate detail. We read in the *Discussion Bulletin* of April 1950, this
account of Yugoslavian events:

> Attempting to fight their way out of their economic cul-de-
> sac by "building socialism in one country," they embarked
> on vastly ambitious plans of industrialization. Since they
> lacked the machinery, resources, productive capacities or
> trained personnel, they began taking it out of the hides of
> the workers. Piecework and speed up were introduced in
> the plants, hours of work lengthened, the authority of man-
> agement made absolute. The desperate nature of the diffi-
> culties was highlighted recently when in Yugoslavia, where
> there exists, in contradistinction to the satellite states, some
> enthusiasm for the plan, the regime was forced to give up
> the "voluntary labor brigade" system and institute a new
> system of contract labor which freezes the worker to his job.

There is no room for disagreement. And here we ask our trade union
comrades particularly to define the system so well described by the
Yugoslavs themselves and by Comrade E.R. Frank. Do they think that
this is a workers' state? Do they think that this is a transitional economy?
How is it distinguished from the conditions of labor in the factories of
the rest of the capitalist world?

Recognition that the Tito regime had suppressed the mass movement was not confined to individual writers. An official statement, ap-
pearing in the *Fourth International* as late as October 1949, was brutal
in its accuracy.

The revolutionary origins of the present regime in Yugoslavia offer a strange contrast to its bureaucratic and monolithic form of rule. What is the reason for this contradictory development? At first glance it would appear that the vast movement of the masses set in motion during the war should have produced a flowering of workers' democracy. But just the contrary occurred. The regime is dominated by a monolithic Stalinist party which imitates the Russian leader cult, boasts of its ruthless suppression of factions and prohibits all vital criticism and opposition to its basic policies.

The statement was equally remorseless in tracing the Stalinist roots of the CPY leadership:

This development has its roots in the history of the Communist Party of Yugoslavia. Beginning as a mass party after the October Revolution, it was stultified by the imposition of false policies and bureaucratic methods from the Stalinized Comintern. In 1937, on orders from the Kremlin, the entire central committee of the party with the exception of Tito was purged. The new leadership was trained in Moscow or in the GPU school in Spain. Taking advantage of the conditions of illegality and official repression, it consolidated its bureaucratic grip on the organization by the suppression of all other tendencies and by framing up and expelling its opponents and critics.

The Titoists, the statement continues, were ruthlessly bureaucratic, particularly against independent revolutionary expressions from the Left:

It was this Stalinized party which succeeded in gaining the leadership of the partisan insurrection. Despite the participation of masses of workers in revolutionary action, bureaucratic methods were favored by the conditions of foreign occupation and civil war which prevailed in the country. Military discipline and rule-by-command became the accepted mode of procedure and were utilized by the Stalinist leadership to stifle any tendency for greater democracy in the ranks of the party and the mass movement. It appears from a study of the events that while a certain latitude was granted to bourgeois groups and parties, independent revolutionary expressions from the left were mercilessly crushed.

Is this the way that Marxism treats what for it is the greatest event in history, the successful proletarian revolution? Surely "Johnson-Forest" are justified in asking for the re-examination of a theory which imposes such humiliating self-stultification upon those who follow it.

Our Political Views on Yugoslavia

Orthodox Trotskyism in all its tendencies is opposed to our analysis. Its own theory has led it to its present attitude toward the closest association possible to the CPY. This is an action, the majority against us is overwhelming, and Bolshevism demands unity in action. The Fourth International will have to make its experiences. We do not therefore propose to carry on any active discussion on the question, but it is of sufficient importance that all should know exactly what are our political views.

(a) The rulers of Yugoslavia may make gestures, overtures, and even sympathetically consider Trotskyism. It is possible that they may even go to the lengths of organizing around them a Fourth International and acting as its center in the same way as Stalinist Russia has for years acted as the organizing center of the Third International. Every success gained along these lines by orthodox Trotskyism makes only more certain the ultimate price that will be paid. The CPY seeks not the world revolution but the defense of "Communism in a single country, Yugoslavia." At the moment when Yugoslavia's mythical independence will be seen as the hollow fiction that it is, i.e., at the moment of the outbreak of war, the CPY will declare policy in terms of the interests of the particular mass of capital to which it is attached. If it should be on the side of Stalinist Russia, it will call upon the workers inside Russia and all over the world to support the Stalinist regime for the purpose of winning victory. If it is on the side of American imperialism, it will summon the proletariat of the United States to work and fight with all its soul for American democracy. At that time it will be able to hit the Fourth International a mighty blow. The Fourth International in return will be able to call the CPY traitors. To have to do that will harm the Fourth International, especially if the present course is continued. It will not harm Titoism in any way.

(b) The past record of the CPY is a record of unwavering support of Stalinist Russia and the Communist International. It has supported Stalinism in its persecution of the Russian workers, its slave labor camps, its Moscow Trials, its monumental lies, its betrayal of proletarian revolution, its sacrificing of the proletariat of whole nations, its assassinations, its incalculable contributions to the barbarism which is now eating away at human society.

The conception that "Johnson-Forest" have of the Fourth International does not include collaboration with these elements but has always seen them as the worst enemies of the proletariat and the organic foes of everything for which the Fourth International must stand.

We do not say that all who have supported Stalinism in the past are unfit for membership in our organization. Members of the GPU have in the past broken with Stalinism and joined the Fourth International. However, as we wrote in 1949:

As with self-determination, the evaluation of Tito's defiance of Stalinism is rooted in the sociological conditions. Mobilization of a mass Communist Party even by Togliatti or Thorez in defiance of the Cominform or the Russian regime would be an event of world-wide significance for the revolutionary movement, however empirical, limited or halting might be the ideological basis on which such a defiance might begin. The defiance by the Yugoslav Communist Party is of a fundamentally different character. It is and cannot be seen otherwise than as a defense of the possession of the state property, control of the surplus-labor and other bureaucratic privileges, on the one hand,

and on the other, fear of being submitted to the ruthless purges of the GPU.

The Titoists are a privileged section of society, exploiting millions of workers and peasants, masters of a state. Their Leninism is neither more nor less than the "Leninism" of Stalinism. Our hostility to them is more implacable than to those Stalinist leaders who are at the head of the proletariat in a country where the proletariat is free to act.[3]

(c) It is our opinion that the whole past of our movement and our whole experience with our opposition to Stalinism should teach us to train our membership and those who listen to us in a spirit of critical hostility, reserve, distrust of all such elements. If their orientation is toward breaking with Stalinist theory and Stalinist practice in deeds and not only in words, that will not be diverted by the harshest criticism from the Trotskyist movement. Undoubtedly Tito's break with Stalin has deeply affected many rank and file elements in the Stalinist parties all over the world. Our intervention should have been our principles, our ideas, in irreconcilable opposition to Titoism. This would have given revolutionary clarification to the dissidents. We are opposed to the defense of Yugoslavia against Stalinist Russia for reasons which we shall explain in the next section. But it was quite possible to combine the defense of the national independence of Yugoslavia against Stalinist Russia with the most critical attitude to the falsity and hypocrisy of Titoist theory and practice. The idea that Tito's declaration in favor of Leninism— and these are nothing to the declarations of Stalin in favor of Leninism—to declare that this is the greatest event in the history of Trotskyism so far, and the hope of our movement for the future,

---

3   Here, regretfully, for it is painful to have to repeat elementary principles of revolutionary practice, we have to recall another aspect of Leninism for those sowers of confusion regarding "Johnson-Forest" critical support to workers' parties which are "agents of a capitalist-Fascist power." We remind these comrades that Lenin's analysis of the Social-Democracy as capitalist parties based on monopoly capitalism, agents of the capitalist national state, did not prevent him from critical support to these parties under certain concrete circumstances where the proletariat was free to act.

is to strike a terrible blow at all that we have stood for in the past. The future of the Fourth International rests, as it has always rested, upon the progress we have made with the revolutionary proletariat in irreconcilable struggle with bureaucracies of all and every kind.

(d) The reports of capable people who have gone to Yugoslavia and returned say that there is "democracy." We can fill notebooks with the views of those who went to Russia and saw the same when the Left Opposition was being hooted down in party meetings. It is possible that everyone discusses Trotskyism freely when the leaders are discussing Trotskyism freely. But Tito has himself given his definition of democratic centralism in his report to the party in 1948. It is that ". . . almost every factionalist is not far from being a provocateur or similar enemy of the working class." "Johnson-Forest" know that this "democratic centralism" can serve only to protect the interests of rulers. If that is wrong, then everything we have been taught and learned is wrong, and we have to begin all over again. However great our differences with Trotsky, we see nothing in his writings to make us believe that he would not have known the difference between an orientation to the bureaucracy of Yugoslavia and an orientation toward the proletarian masses and poor peasants of that country.

X
Some Political Conclusions

STATE CAPITALISM, I.E., the result of the world tendency to *centralization*, so powerful in Europe, has brought with it not only a labor bureaucracy determined to destroy the national state. A glance at Europe today will show how altered are the conditions from those which existed as late as 1940. In 1947 in *The Invading Socialist Society*, we wrote as the second of the two points which summed up our ideas: "II. THE STRATEGIC ORIENTATION IS THE UNIFICATION OF PROLETARIAN STRUGGLE ON AN INTERNATIONAL SCALE AS EXEMPLIFIED IN THE STRUGGLE FOR THE SOCIALIST UNITED STATES OF EUROPE."

At the World Congress in 1948, our European co-thinkers presented no separate resolution on Russia. For them, as for us, that is over. They presented one resolution for the whole international situation and on the Russian discussion presented for voting merely extracts from the international resolution. The point of view may be gathered from this brief extract from the resolution:

> Today the movement toward the centralization of European capital, which ensured the victory of statified property against the kulak, has solidified the power of the bureaucracy at home and projected its state and its army into the heart of Europe, in the interlude of peace as well as in war. Once more, in World War II, the great masses of the Russian peasantry, organized in the army, were injected into the political struggles of Europe, this time as far as Berlin. Despite withdrawals, substantial elements have been left there and tomorrow will be reinforced by even greater numbers. Great numbers of the European proletariat are under essentially Russian domination. Great numbers of the advanced proletariat of Germany and the rest of Europe have been conversely incorporated

into all levels of the proletariat in the gangrenous society of Russia. Only a perspective of the complete defeat of the proletariat and the reversal of bourgeois society to outmoded forms (the theory of retrogression) can therefore see as the axis of policy the danger of the restoration of private property in this struggle of the Russian proletariat against the Russian bureaucracy, in peace or in war.

The resolution analyzed the European socialist character of the coming Russian Revolution:

> The Russian struggle is in reality the struggle between the Russian proletariat and the Russian bureaucracy for the control of the Russian statified economy and for the emancipation or enslavement of the labor movement of Europe and Eastern Asia. In 1929 the pressure of world capital compelled the bureaucracy to side with the proletariat against the kulak. Today the centralization of European capital and the penetration of the Red Army into the heart of Europe has thrown into insignificance the danger of the kulak restoration. The Russian proletariat and the masses of peasants organized in the Red Army have become an integral part of the concrete struggle on a European scale for the revolutionary seizure of power and its uninterrupted transformation into socialist revolution. The task today and tomorrow is the integration of the European proletarian revolutionary forces, particularly in Eastern and Central Europe, with the Russian proletariat. Inside Russia and outside, the great oppressed masses of Europe, burning with indignation at the totalitarian apparatus, will seek to split the great masses of the Russian peasants and workers from the MVD, the Kremlin bureaucracy, the officer caste and their bureaucratic colonial satellites.

Never was the perspective of world revolution so concrete:

> If World War III is not prevented by proletarian revolution and takes its projected course, the vast millions of the basic

revolutionary forces in Europe will more or less rapidly be transformed into an international army of resistance movements. The revolutionary vanguard, steeled by the conviction that humanity moves inexorably and concretely to the proletarian power on a world scale, or universal ruin, sinks itself deeper and deeper into the mass movement, preparing the proletariat for the vast revolutionary upheavals on a continental scale which it knows must come, in peace or in war. In the present conditions of Europe, any policy which impedes, confuses or deflects the proletariat from this course in peace or in war can have ruinous consequences for that party which is responsible for them.

It is from our economic analysis also that we judge the present tendencies in world politics: the politics of the atomic and hydrogen bombs and the Berlin air-lift; the domination of Eastern Europe by Russia; the Marshall Plan, the division and occupation of Germany, the Truman Doctrine, Truman's program for sending capital to underdeveloped countries, the end of isolationism in the U.S., the international activities of the CIO and the AFL, the Assembly for a United Europe, to which must be added the hopeless economic situation of China and other colonial areas without aid, economic, social and political, from the proletariat of the advanced countries. That is why in the resolution previously referred to there appeared the following:

> As far back as 1932, Trotsky in the face of the German counter-revolution, urged upon the Left Opposition the publication and popularization of a plan for the joint proletarian development of German and Russian economy. In a world situation in which even the bourgeoisie must envisage and as far as possible plan the reorganization of economy on a continental and world scale, the Fourth International has remained helpless and impotent before this responsibility which it and it alone can carry out.
>
> Since 1943 the Fourth International has been ceaselessly warned of the necessity for giving as concrete an expression as possible to the slogan of the Socialist United

States of Europe. Precisely because of its complete failure to do this, it has suffered and continues to suffer a series of terrible blows.

(a) It has allowed the bourgeoisie and the Stalinist bureaucracy to take the initiative by a spurious, counter-revolutionary but at any rate concrete "internationalism."

(b) It leaves the European proletariat politically disarmed before the vigorous theoretical and practical intervention of the American bourgeoisie and the Kremlin into every aspect of European economy and politics.

(c) Lacking a concrete plan of its own in opposition to the Marshall Plan, it not only allows the labor administrators of American capital to pose as the apostles of internationalism and proletarian aid. By the abstractness of its posing of the strategy of the Socialist United States of Europe, it is reduced to a shameful tail ending of the powerful Stalinist opposition and still further encourages pro-Stalinist tendencies.

(d) The absence of a plan which includes the Russian economy under the control of the Russian proletariat leaves the Russian proletariat, the proletariat of Eastern Europe and the Russian occupation troops without a glimpse of a perspective opposed to the two imperialisms and still further facilitates the penetration into the movement of the unparalleled lies and falsifications of Stalinist propaganda.

The resolution stressed the interpenetration of imperialist and civil wars in our epoch, in Europe, Asia and Africa, and warned that only the concrete strategy of coordinating the revolutionary actions of the oppressed masses across national lines would advance the proletarian revolution:

It is the task of the Fourth International carefully to watch each concrete situation and to safeguard the proletarian vanguard from committing itself to support of the Russian regime or to opposition movements, disguised as national movements which are in reality agents of American imperialism. Without missing one opportunity of tactical support of any section of the *oppressed masses* in its concrete struggle against oppression, the Fourth International bases its policy on the concrete stage of development and strives in peace as well as in war to unite the revolutionary elements in both camps. In areas like Eastern Europe, the objective situation demands that the workers base their revolutionary policy on the unification of the oppressed masses in both the oppressing and the oppressed countries against the oppressing powers. The same basic strategy must guide the Fourth International in Korea and Manchuria.

The resolution included a special warning on colonial revolutions in our epoch:

> The experience of China indicates the economic perils of colonial revolution in the age when the export of surplus capital has practically come to an end. After nearly forty years of unceasing civil war, the economy of the country is falling to pieces. The socialist economic reconstruction of China, integrated with the industrial potential of Japan and Manchuria, must form the fundamental theoretical basis of the struggle against the native bourgeoisie and the imperialism of the U.S. and Russia. Vast revolutionary movements in Africa and historical and geographical conditions similarly link the struggle for the Socialist United States of Africa to the European and world economy.

The same tendency to centralization explains our opposition to the support of the struggle for the national independence of Yugoslavia. We did not arrive at this when Tito broke with Stalin. In 1947, in *The Invading Socialist Society* (31), we explained with great care why for Poland, Czechoslovakia, Yugoslavia, Rumania and Hungary, the struggle for national independence since World War II is an illusion and cannot fail to have reactionary consequences.[1]

The same centralization, state-capitalism and the capitalist bureaucracy it brings, also determines what was expressed as follows:

> In France and Italy any movement of the masses brings them immediately into direct conflict with their own leaders

---

1   Reprinted in *A New Notion: Two Works by C.L.R. James* (Oakland: PM Press, 2010).

as rulers or direct representatives of the government. The simplest of the immediate demands concerning the high cost of living or the right to strike become questions of state policy and continually pose before the workers the fundamental question of state power. Thus the social structure of state power in statified production places the workers in a situation where any determined struggle compels them to face the problem of creating their own organization in order to bring pressure upon, and if necessary, to break the power of the labor leadership as virtual functionaries of the existing government.... Every crisis of production, whether resulting in increase or decrease of wages, becomes merely an opportunity of the bourgeois state, behind constitutional forms, to limit and circumscribe the most elementary rights, right to strike, etc., of the masses. Thus, the struggle for democracy, particularly in advanced countries, is no longer the struggle for the extension of popular rights. Liberalism is now the advocate, instead of the enemy of states (Wallace). ... Thus, in the statified production, the constant struggle for democratic rights becomes the struggle for militant independent mass organizations by which the workers can mobilize themselves to bring pressure upon, control, renew and ultimately overthrow the trade union bureaucracy and the labor leadership on the road to the proletarian revolution. This is the strategic basis for the tactical orientation toward the struggle for democratic demands in this period.

All these are strategic orientations for an international movement. Practical politics consists of the art of applying them in infinitely varied circumstances, but the variety is in the circumstances, not in what is to be applied. It is our opinion that to point, on the one hand, to the contemporary barbarism, the imminent destruction of civilization and not to put the boldest program concretely before the masses is equivalent to saying that *they* do not yet understand the nature of the modern crisis. We believe that they understand it better than any other section of the population, taught by the very structure and insoluble contradictions of state-capitalism.

XI
Philosophy and State Capitalism

WHEN WE REACH state-capitalism, one-party state, cold war, hydrogen bomb, it is obvious that we have reached ultimates. We are now at the stage where all universal questions are matters of concrete specific urgency for society in general as well as for every individual. As we wrote in *The Invading Socialist Society*: "It is precisely the character of our age and the maturity of humanity that obliterates the opposition between theory and practice, between the intellectual occupations of the 'educated' and the masses" (14).

All previous distinctions, politics and economics, war and peace, agitation and propaganda, party and mass, the individual and society, national, civil and imperialist war, single country and one world, immediate needs and ultimate solutions—all these it is impossible to keep separate any longer. Total planning is inseparable from permanent crisis, the world struggle for the minds of men from the world tendency to the complete mechanization of men.

State-capitalism is in itself *the* total contradiction, absolute antagonism. In it are concentrated all the contradictions of revolution and counter-revolution. The proletariat, never so revolutionary as it is today, is over half the world in the stranglehold of Stalinism, the form of the counter-revolution in our day, the absolute opposite of the proletarian revolution.

It is the totality of these contradictions that today compels philosophy, a total conception. Hence the propaganda ministry of Hitler, the omnipresent orthodoxy of Stalinism, the Voice of America. The war over productivity is fought in terms of philosophy, a way of life. When men question not the fruits of toil but the toil itself, then philosophy in Marx's sense of human activity has become actual.

World War I plunged the world into complete chaos. Lenin between 1914 and 1917 established in theory: (a) the economic basis of the counter-revolutionary Social Democracy (The economic basis of imperialist war had been established before him.); (b) the Soviet democracy in contradistinction to bourgeois democracy. But before he did this, he had to break with the philosophical method of the Second International. He worked at this privately in a profound study of the Hegelian dialectic applied to Marx's *Capital*, the proletarian revolution and the dictatorship of the proletariat.

Thirty years have now passed. Lenin's *method* of economic analysis is ours to use, not to repeat his findings. His *political* conception of complete abolition of bureaucracy and all ordering from above is today to be driven to its ultimate as the revolutionary weapon against the one-party state. But today the problems of *production* which Lenin had to tackle in Russia in 1920 are *universal*. No longer to be ignored is the philosophical method he used in holding fast to the creation of a new and higher social organization of labor as "the essence" of the dictatorship of the proletariat. It is not the Marxists who have compelled society to face this issue. Today in every layer of society, the great philosophical battles that matter are precisely those over production, the role of the proletariat, the one-party state, and many of the combatants are professed dialecticians.

The crisis of production today is the crisis of the antagonism between manual and intellectual labor. The problem of modern philosophy from Descartes in the sixteenth century to Stalinism in 1950 is the problem of the division of labor between the intellectuals and the workers.

Rationalism: The Philosophy of the Bourgeoisie

The revolutionary bourgeoisie which established its power against feudalism could only develop a philosophy of history and of society in which, on the one hand, it spoke for the progress of all society, and on the other, for itself as the leaders of society. This philosophy can be summed up in one word: rationalism.

Rationalism is the philosophy of bourgeois political economy. It is materialist and not idealist in so far as it combats superstition, seeks to expand the productive forces and increase the sum total of goods. But there is no such thing as a classless materialism. Rationalism conceives this expansion as a division of labor between the passive masses and the active elite. Thereby it reinstates idealism. Because it does not and cannot doubt that harmonious progress is inevitable by this path, the essence of rationalism is uncritical or vulgar materialism, and uncritical or vulgar idealism.

In the springtime of capitalism this rationalistic division of labor was the basis of a common attempt of individual men associated *in a natural environment to achieve control over nature*. Today this division of labor is the *control in social production* of the administrative elite *over the masses*. Rationalism has reached its end in the complete divorce and absolute disharmony between manual and intellectual labor, between the socialized proletariat and the monster of centralized capital.

The specific political ideology developed by rationalism was democracy—equality of opportunity for all men to rise to the top, and hence equality in all spheres outside of production, before the law, at the polls and in the market.

Today, from end to end of the world, men know that democracy is bankrupt. What is to take its place they do not know. The alternative seems to be planned economy and one-party state. This is *the* philosophical question.

But the philosophy of planned economy and one-party state is distinguishable from that of the bourgeoisie only by its more complete rationalism. The labor bureaucracy in power or out of it sees the solution to the crisis of production in scientific progress, greater output. It consciously seeks to plan and organize the division of labor as the means to further accumulation of capital. In ideology it is ready to expropriate those representatives of private property who stand in the way of this complete rationalization.

But didn't this bureaucracy develop out of the working class? It did and it could only have developed out of the working class. It is a product of the modern mass movement, created by the centralization of capital, and holds its position only because of this movement. At the same time it cannot conceive the necessity for abolishing the division of labor in production, the only solution to the crisis in production. By a remorseless logic, therefore, representation of the proletariat turns into its opposite, administration over the proletariat. The end of bourgeois rationalism is this crisis of the revolution and counter-revolution in production.

The Hegelian Critique of Rationalism

There are various critiques of rationalism. *All* base themselves on Hegel. *All* are primarily concerned with the proletariat.

Until the epoch of the French Revolution, the philosophy of uncritical materialism and uncritical idealism was not seriously challenged. It was the emergence of the active masses in the French Revolution, on the one hand, and on the other, the counter-revolution carried to its completion by Napoleon, which created a crisis in this ideology.

As early as 1781, a challenge to rationalism had already come from backward Germany. For the French and English petty-bourgeoisie, rationalism had a material base, the advances of modern industry. The powerless German petty-bourgeoisie, however, could criticize rationalism because for them it was only theory. Kant's *Critique of Pure Reason* posed the contradiction between advancing science and human freedom. It was the first introduction into the modern world of dialectic which begins with the recognition of contradiction. But Kant wrote before the French Revolution and Napoleon. He could therefore believe in the solution of the contradiction by a moral elite, all men who obeyed the moral law of acting in accordance with the general interest. The uncritical or vulgar idealism of rationalism was replaced by critical or moral idealism.

Hegel, on the other hand, having seen the revolution and counter-revolution, could entertain no such reliance on men of goodwill. He began by placing contradiction squarely in the center of reality. Thereby he rejected rationalism, either in its traditional bourgeois form or its petty-bourgeois Kantian variation. Hegel refused even to argue with anybody who doubted that contradictions are real.

In brief, Hegel's critique of rationalism asserts:

(a) Contradiction, *not* harmonious increase and decrease, is the creative and moving principle of history. Society cannot develop unless it has to overcome contradiction.

(b) All development takes place as a result of *self*-movement, *not* organization or direction by external forces.

(c) Self-movement springs from and is the overcoming of antagonisms *within* an organism, *not* the struggle against external foes.

(d) It is *not* the world of nature that confronts man as an alien power to be overcome. It is the alien power that he has himself created.

(e) The end toward which mankind is inexorably developing by the constant overcoming of internal antagonisms is *not* the enjoyment, ownership or use of goods, but self-realization, creativity based upon the incorporation into the individual personality of the whole previous development of humanity. Freedom is creative universality, *not* utility. Between 1914 and 1917 Lenin, for the first time, mastered this.

These dialectical principles which were the heart of Hegel's system are absolutely revolutionary. After the French Revolution, no further progress in thought could be made without holding fast to the principle of creativity and the contradictory process by which this creativity develops. The next step forward in human thought had to be the appropriation of these principles by the revolutionary masses, dialectical materialism. Any other path meant barbarism and intellectual disintegration. The Paris Commune and Marx's *Capital*, these are the heights reached by society in the nineteenth century. On the other side, what? Cavaignac, Napoleon III, Bismarck; Baudelaire, Dostoevsky, Rimbaud, the counter-revolutionary regime of state-capital and the desperate soul-searching intellectuals.

It is fashionable to use Marx's statement that he stood Hegel on his head to transform Marx into a vulgar materialist preoccupied with technological progress and the stomachs of the masses, expanded production and increased consumption. It is today the most dangerous perversion of all Marx stood for. Marx himself in his fight against vulgar materialism reaffirmed that "the Hegelian contradiction (is) the source of all dialectic." Without the dialectic of Hegel, the idealism of Hegel could not be destroyed. But the dialectic of Hegel could be retained and expanded only by the concept of the creative activity of the masses. On this basis the dialectic became in Marx's hands a revolutionary theoretical weapon against bureaucracy in all its forms, but primarily and particularly in the process of production.

As we wrote in *World Revolutionary Perspectives*:

Hegel saw objective history as the successive manifestation of a world-spirit. Marx placed the objective movement in the process of production. Hegel had been driven to see the perpetual quest for universality as necessarily confined to the process of knowledge. Marx reversed this and rooted the quest for universality in the need for the free and full development of all the inherent and acquired characteristics in productive and intellectual labor. Hegel had made the motive force of history the work of a few gifted individuals in whom was concentrated the social movement. Marx propounded the view that it was only when ideas seized hold of the masses that the process of history moved. Hegel dreaded the revolt of the modem mass. Marx made the modern proletarian revolution the motive force of modem history. Hegel placed the guardianship of society in the hands of the bureaucracy. Marx saw future society as headed for ruin except under the rulership of the proletariat and the vanishing distinction between intellectual and manual labor (xx).

Hegel could not carry the dialectical logic to its conclusions in the socialist revolution because he did not and could not base himself on the advanced industrial proletariat. He saw and described with horror the fragmentation and loss of individuality by the worker under the capitalist division of labor. But the workers whom he knew were not the organized, disciplined and united proletariat which had by Marx's time begun to announce itself as the new organizer of society and which we know so well today.

Hegel could not know these and therefore he could not envisage universal freedom for the masses of men. The result was that in politics, economics and philosophy, he was compelled to reinstate the old rationalistic division of labor between the intellectual elite and the masses. Hegel did not only imply this. He stated it. The universal bureaucratic class, the intellectual class, must rule society. Again, as we wrote in *World Revolutionary Perspectives*:

Concrete universality for the mass of men was impossible. It was a mighty decision to take. But Hegel did not flinch.

Only the state, said Hegel, could embody universality for the community. But *in particular* the state was a defense against the revolutionary masses. Hegel had seen them and their activities in European history and now the French Revolution had shown that nothing could ever come of it. So it had been and it would ever be. At each stage, therefore, a few chosen individuals represented the abstract spirit of mankind. Universality had to be restricted to these. This was the basis of Hegel's idealism. But with the clear insight of a great scholar of both past and contemporary history, and by his mastery of his method, he analyzed and drew his analysis to its conclusions. The state would have to organize production. The chaos of capitalist production would have to be disciplined by organizing the separate industries into corporations. The state would be the state of the corporations. Universality being impossible to all men, the state bureaucracy would embody universality and represent the community (xix).

So that in the end, the greatest of all the bourgeois philosophers, the most encyclopedic mind that Europe had produced, the founder of the dialectic, in Engels' words, the maker of an epoch, could not transcend his historic barrier and was recaptured in the rationalist trap from which he had sought so profoundly to extricate European thought. Hegel destroyed all dogmatisms but one—the dogmatism of the backwardness of the masses. Once the revolutionary solution of the contradiction escaped him, he clung to the bureaucracy. The intellectual elite would rescue society and discipline the revolting masses. Reinstated were uncritical materialism, a purely material existence for the masses, and uncritical idealism, the solution of social crisis by the intellectual bureaucracy.

We today who have seen Stalinism and the labor bureaucracy the world over can first fully comprehend this, Marx's essential critique of Hegel.[1] Only the revolutionary proletariat, said Marx, can appropriate

---

1 "Critique of the Hegelian Dialectic," *Three Essays by Karl Marx, Selected from the Economic-Philosophical Manuscripts*, 31; *Critique of the Hegelian Philosophy of Right, Marx-Engels Gesamtausgabe*, Abt. 1, Bd. 1, 1st Halbband. For English extract, see *World Revolutionary Perspectives*, xxi onward.

the dialectical logic of Hegel. Hegel himself, because he held fast to the intellectual elite, ended up, despite his thoroughgoing analysis of contradiction and negativity, in the crass materialism and crass idealism of the state bureaucracy.

Today Hegel's idealism or Marx's dialectical materialism are no longer theory. The elite, the organizers, the administrators, the leaders, confront the self-mobilized proletariat. Counter-revolution and revolution oppose one another without intermediaries. Modern society offers no third camp between complete totalitarianism and complete democracy.

Rationalism: The Philosophy of Stalinism

The philosophy of Stalinism is the philosophy of the elite, the bureaucracy, the organizers, the leaders, clothed in Marxist terminology. It is the extreme, the historical limit of the rationalism of the bourgeoisie, carefully organized to look like a new revolutionary doctrine.

Stalinism, the ideology of state-capitalism, is the reinstatement of uncritical materialism and uncritical idealism. The materialism is in the accumulation theory: the kernel of all Stalinist-Titoist philosophy is that the worker must work harder than he ever did before. The idealism is in the theory of the party: the leaders, the elite, must lead as they never did before.

No one is more conscious of this than the Stalinist bureaucracy itself. At the center of all ideological campaigns in Stalinist Russia is the attitude of the workers toward their work: "People . . . consider labor as something alien to them . . . regard their work joylessly or indifferently . . . contrive to give society less output and worse quality and to take from the government and from society as much as they can."

The Stalinists call these workers: "our loafers, our triflers, our grabbers, flouting labor discipline, looking sullenly askance at their work—which leads to flaws in output, to damaged equipment and tools, to breakdown in production schedules, and to other *negative* manifestations which retard the increase of production."[2]

---

2   S. Kovalyov, "Communist Education of the Worker and the Elimination of Capitalist Survivals from the Popular Consciousness," published as *Ideological Conflicts in Soviet Russia* (Washington, DC: Public Affairs Press, 1948) (emphasis added).

For the Stalinist bureaucracy, state-property converts labor "from the drab burden it was under capitalism into a matter of honor and glory, a matter of prowess and heroism" The intelligentsia tells the workers: You work. The workers, on the other hand, continue to resist speed-up and the discipline of accumulated capital, statified or otherwise. This is called by the Stalinists "the old outlook on labor," a "capitalist survival in the popular consciousness." This is no longer a question of Soviet youth and textbooks in political economy. It is now the workers counterposing to the bureaucracy another "ideology" which the Stalinists admit "may spread to alarming dimensions."

The Stalinists recognize the urgent necessity of mobilizing "all the vehicles of ideological work" to combat this "outlook and conduct" and to "educate the workers in the spirit of self-sacrificing work for the national weal." To the outlook and conduct of the workers, the bureaucracy must counterpose its own outlook and conduct. The conduct is the unbridled savagery of the police-state; the outlook is undisguised rationalism, "a materialistic outlook upon life . . . an exclusively scientific concept of the universe."

In June 1947, the Central Committee of the CPSU withdrew from circulation a textbook on the *History of Western Philosophy* by Georgi Alexandrov, which in 1946 had won a Stalin prize. Zhdanov, who spoke for the Central Committee at a national conference of "philosophical workers," made it clear that philosophy was no longer an "academic" question but of "enormous scientific and political significance."[3] The "gravest dangers" ("much graver than you imagine") threatened unless the philosophical front was reorganized along two main lines: (a) the rewriting of the history of philosophy as the history of science; and (b) the divorce of Marx from Hegel and the purging of Hegel from philosophic discussion. Six months later there appeared an outline of how "A Soviet History of Philosophy" ought to be written.[4]

The main enemy of social progress from the days of the ancient Orient and Greece to the present was discovered to be the idealism of superstition. Revolutionary ideology was equated with the materialism

---

3 A. Zhdanov, "On the History of Philosophy," *Political Affairs* (April 1948): 344–66.
4 Published by the Public Affairs Press, Washington, DC, 1950.

of scientific progress. Quoting Stalin, Marxism was described as retaining only "the rational kernel" of Hegel's dialectic logic, "so as to give it a contemporary scientific appearance."

On the surface it appeared that the Stalinist intervention was to defend the materialism of Marx against the idealism of Hegel. In reality the theoretical threat came from the revolutionary dialectical logic. In political economy the Stalinists seek to defend the classless nature of state-property and planning. The theoretical enemy is the theory of state-capitalism. In philosophy they seek to propagate the fiction of the classless nature of rationalism and materialism. The enemy is the proletariat resisting labor discipline by the bureaucracy.

Again and again Zhdanov attacked Alexandrov for "objectivism." The Stalinists are terrified by the obviously growing conviction that there is in Stalinist Russia an "objective" basis for the "struggle of opposites, the struggle between the old and the new, between the dying and the rising, between the decaying and the developing." Such an objective basis could only be the class struggle. Hence they must purge Marxism of the Hegelian concept of the objectivity of contradiction.

Materialism without the dialectics of objective contradiction is idealism. If development does not take place by the overcoming of objective contradiction, then everything depends on the subject, the leaders, the elite, the bureaucracy. Zhdanov, the vulgar materialist, had therefore to demand that the philosophical workers produce a "new aspect of movement, a new type of development, a new dialectical law." This exceptionally new, exceptionally subjective, revision of Marxism was titled: "Criticism and Self-Criticism: The Special Form of Struggle Between the Old and the New." Zhdanov stated unambiguously the inseparable connection between the new subjectivism and the Stalinist denial of the class struggle in Russia:

> In our Soviet society, where antagonistic classes have been liquidated, the struggle between the old and the new, and consequently the development from the lower to the higher, proceeds not in the form of struggle between antagonistic classes and of cataclysms, as is the case under capitalism, but in the form of criticism and self-criticism, which is the real motive force of our development, a powerful

instrument in the hands of the Party. This is, incontestably, a new aspect of movement, a new type of development, a new dialectical law.

In 1949, the Institute of Philosophy of the Academy of Sciences of the USSR delivered the new ideology which Zhdanov had ordered.[5] The development of Soviet society was identified with the consciousness, the theory, the plan, the policy, the foresight of the Communist Party, the Soviet state. The new idealism was proclaimed unequivocally: "Herein lies the strength and significance of our party, of scientific theory, of socialist consciousness."

The steps of Hegel's decline are here undeviatingly retraced. Hegel, who did not know the socialized proletariat, began by regarding all history as the history of the philosopher, of consciousness and self-consciousness, and ended with the state bureaucracy. The Stalinists use almost the identical phrases.

The proletariat's role in the struggle for socialism is to work harder and harder, while the leadership and organization are left to the "criticism and self-criticism" of the elite, the bureaucracy, the party. Everything depends on the party, on the bureaucracy's consciousness and self-consciousness of correctness and incorrectness, its direction, its control, its foresight. The masses are merely at the disposal of the party as they are at the disposal of capital.

This is the Stalinist philosophy in every sphere, political economy, politics, history, education, literature, art. *The History of the Communist Party of the Soviet Union*, published before World War II, was the first comprehensive statement of the primacy of the party, of political consciousness over objective economic development, applied to the development of Russia before, during and after the revolution. In 1943, *The Teaching of Political Economy in the Soviet Union* was hailed as the reorganization by economists of all their work according to the model of the *History*. Since the end of World War II, and particularly with the philosophic systematization of the new idealism in 1947, the ideological

---

5   Fedor Vasil'evich Konstantinov, *The Role of Socialist Consciousness in the Development of Soviet Society* (Moscow: Foreign Languages Publishing House, 1950).

mobilization of the bureaucracy has been total. The Stalinist bureaucracy unambiguously proclaims the one-party State of the Plan as the vital foundation of the Soviet system.

To believe that this vigorous offensive in every sphere is a question of nationalism is a mistake as crippling as the belief that Stalinism betrays the revolution by social-patriotic support of the national state. In every country the Stalinists represent bureaucratic manipulation of the proletariat by the elite, the bureaucracy, the party. They are the extreme limit of the rationalism of the bourgeoisie, uncritical materialism and uncritical idealism. Never before has so gigantic a state mobilized itself with such murderous vigilance to keep the proletariat at work while the leaders and organizers plan. This is the most deadly enemy the proletariat has ever had. Rationalism and counter-revolution have become one.

The Ideological Crisis of the Intermediate Classes

The totality of the crisis has given manifold forms to the counter-revolution. The most deadly, the most insidious, the most dangerous is the Stalinist counter-revolution because it springs from the proletariat and cloaks itself in Marxist terminology. The most obviously reactionary, the most easily recognizable is the counter-revolution of the middle classes. Because capitalism in its present stage, state-capitalism, faces them with complete liquidation and absorption into the proletariat, they propose the complete destruction of capitalism and return to a new medievalism, based on natural inequality. This is the program of the Christian Humanists, militantly anti-rationalist, militantly anti-democratic.

Like all forms of anti-rationalism, Christian Humanism leans heavily upon the Hegelian dialectic. The Hegelian concept of objective contradiction—the source of all dialectic—is transformed into a subjective conflict in the individual between sin and salvation, between individual imperfection and divine perfection. The crisis is moral and the solution must be moral, faith in divine authority.

The Christian Humanists describe with brutal accuracy and prophetic dread the fragmentation of the workers in large-scale production and therein the threat to the very life of society. Nothing else could give them their crusading obsession that rationalism has reached its ultimate, the destruction of society itself. But the Christian Humanists cannot see the proletarian solution. That is the hopeless dilemma out of which they have created a philosophy of complete regression to religious idealism.

The Christian Humanists have a systematic political economy. They propose decentralized self-governing corporations of private property with every worker in his place. They have a philosophy of history. They believe in the eternal ambiguities of the human situation and the impossibility of ever attaining human freedom on earth. They have a theory of politics. The natural and ideological elite must rule, the masses must not have absolute sovereignty. Since evil and imperfection are eternal, they say, the alternatives are either limited sovereignty or unmitigated authoritarianism.

These are the philosophic values which have helped de Gasperi in Italy and the MRP and de Gaulle in France to rally around them the desperate middle classes. In increasing numbers, established university intellectuals in the United States are attracted to the same conceptions, radiating from the University of Chicago. There are individual nuances among the Christian Humanists, but as an all-embracing philosophy, Christian Humanism prepares the middle classes to resist to the end the proletarian revolution and to adapt themselves at decisive moments to Fascism. (Of this Rauschning in Germany has given eloquent testimony.) Hence, it is a useful weapon in the hands of big business and the diminishing magnates, so diminished today that more than ever they are dependent upon the middle classes for a mass base. In the United States, the Christian Humanists (for example, Peter Drucker) will join with the labor bureaucracy to keep the mass of workers in their place at the base of the hierarchy in production.

For the workers Christian Humanism is no problem. Their degradation in production goes far beyond the moral capacity of any individual to aggravate or alleviate. They attack the labor bureaucracy for precisely that for which the Christian Humanists support it. However, for seducing intellectuals by the wholesale repudiation of rationalism and for attracting them to Fascism, Christian Humanism plays an important role in the war of ideologies springing from the total crisis in production today.

The rationalism of the bourgeoisie has ended in the Stalinist one-party bureaucratic-administrative state of the Plan. In their repulsion from this rationalism and from the proletarian revolution, the middle classes fall back upon the barbarism of Fascism. The anti-Stalinist, anti-capitalist petty-bourgeois intellectuals, themselves the victims of the absolute division between mental and physical labor, do not know where to go or what to do. Unable to base themselves completely upon the modern proletariat, they turn inward, pursuing a self-destructive, soul-searching analysis of their own isolation, alienation and indecision. They too appropriate the Hegelian dialectic, interpreting it as an unceasing conflict in the individual between affirmation and negation, between deciding for and deciding against.

These intellectuals are the most cultivated in the modern world, in the sense of knowing the whole past of human culture. Having achieved what the idealism of Hegel posed as the Absolute, they are undergoing a theoretical disintegration without parallel in human history. In France this disintegration has assumed the form of a literary movement, Existentialism. In America it takes the form of a mania for psychoanalysis, reaching in to all layers of society but nowhere more than among the most urbane, sensitive and cultivated individuals. In Germany the intellectuals cannot choose between Christian Humanism and psychoanalysis, whether guilt or sickness is the root of the German catastrophe. This is total unreason, the disintegration of a society without values or perspective, the final climax to centuries of division of labor between the philosophers and the proletarians.

Philosophy Must Become Proletarian

There is no longer any purely *philosophical* answer to all this. These philosophical questions, and very profound they are, Marxism says can be solved *only* by the revolutionary action of the proletariat and the masses. There is and can be no other answer. As we have said, we do not propose to do right what the Stalinists have failed to do or do wrong.

Progress in Russia, says Zhdanov, is criticism and self-criticism. The state owns the property, therefore the proletariat must work and work and work. The proletarian revolution alone will put state-property in its place.

In the United States the bourgeoisie extols all the advantages of democracy, the bureaucracy those of science. The proletarian revolution alone will put science in its place and establish complete democracy.

The evils that Christian Humanism sees, the problem of alienation, of mechanized existence, the alienated Existentialist, the alienated worker, internationalism, peace—all are ultimate problems and beyond the reach of any *ideological* solution.

The revolution, the mass proletarian revolution, the creativity of the masses, everything begins here. This is Reason today. The great philosophical problems have bogged down in the mire of Heidegger, Existentialism, psychoanalysis, or are brutally "planned" by the bureaucracies. They can be solved only in the revolutionary reason of the masses. This is what Lenin made into a universal as early as the 1905 Revolution: "The point is that it is precisely the revolutionary periods that are distinguished for their greater breadth, greater wealth, greater intelligence, greater and more systematic activity, greater audacity and vividness of historical creativeness, compared with periods of philistine, Cadet reformist progress."

He drove home the opposition between bourgeois reason and proletariat reason:

> But Mr. Blank and Co. picture it the other way about. They
> pass off poverty as historical-creative wealth. They regard
> the inactivity of the suppressed, downtrodden masses as
> the triumph of the "systematic" activity of the bureaucrats
> and the bourgeoisie. They shout about the disappearance
> of sense and reason, when the picking to pieces of parlia-
> mentary bills by all sorts of bureaucrats and liberal "penny
> a-liners" gives way to a period of direct political activity by
> the "common people," who in their simple way directly and
> immediately destroy the organs of oppression of the peo-
> ple, seize power, appropriate for themselves what was con-
> sidered to be the property of all sorts of plunderers of the
> people—in a word, precisely when the sense and reason of
> millions of downtrodden people is awakening, not only for
> reading books but for action, for living human action, for
> historical creativeness. (*Selected Works*, Vol. VII, 261)

That was the first Russian Revolution. In the Second the proletariat created the form of its political and social rule. Now the whole development of the objective situation demands the fully liberated historical creativeness of the masses, *their* sense and reason, a new and higher organization of labor, new social ties, associated humanity. That is the solution to the problems of production and to the problems of philosophy. Philosophy must become proletarian.

Yet there is a philosophical task in itself strictly philosophical. The doctrine of negativity and the whole system of Hegel, the specific doctrines of Marx, philosophical, political economy, party, all are geared to precisely this situation, this impasse in every sphere which only the proletarian revolution can solve. This is the task today, and politically and philosophically you cannot separate it from production. The field is open, the proletariat, in so far as it is ready to listen, is willing to hear this. Organized schools of bourgeois thought are vulnerable from head to foot. In France, philosophers, historians, scientists, and writers are active protagonists in heated debates over humanism (is it the total rationalism of Stalinism, or Christian Humanism, or Existentialism?); which of the three is the heir to Hegel?

Often intellectuals turn toward Marx and Lenin and Hegel. They meet Stalinism which *spends incredible time, care, energy and vigilance in holding Marx and Lenin within the bounds of their private-property state-property philosophy.* The Stalinists repeat interminably that dialectics is the transformation of quantity into quality, leaps, breaks in continuity, opposition of capitalism and socialism. It is part and parcel of their determination to represent state-property as revolutionary. In 1917, when the struggle in the working class movement was between reform and revolution, these conceptions may have been debatable. Today all arguments fade into insignificance in face of the actuality. The critical question today, which the Stalinists must avoid like the revolution, is how was the October Revolution transformed into its opposite, the Stalinist counter-revolution, and how is this counter-revolution in turn to be transformed into its opposite. This is the dialectical law which Lenin mastered between 1914 and 1917, the negation of the negation, the self-mobilization of the proletariat as the economics and politics of socialism.

The Stalinist bureaucracy is determined that not a hint of the revolutionary doctrines of Hegel, Marx, Lenin should ever go out without *its* imprint, *its* interpretation. The social cooperativeness and unity of modern labor does not allow it any laxity from its cruel and merciless state-capitalist need to make the workers work harder and harder. No hint of the *revolutionary* struggle against bureaucracy must come to workers or to questing intellectuals. Yet every strand of Marx's and Lenin's methodology, philosophy, political economy, lead today directly to the destruction of bureaucracy as such.

Some petty-bourgeois professors and students, theoretically, in history, philosophy and literature, are struggling through to a Marxist solution. The proletariat constantly tries to create itself as the state, i.e., no state at all. But Stalinism is the deadly enemy of both. It is the armed conscious active counter-revolution.

The proletariat, like every organism, must from itself and its conditions develop its own antagonisms and its own means of overcoming them. Stalinism is the decay of world capitalism, a state-capitalism within the proletariat itself and is in essence no more than an expression within the proletariat of the violent and insoluble tensions of capitalism at the stage of state-capitalism. One of the most urgent tasks is to trace the evolution of the counter-revolution within the revolution, from liberalism through anarchism, Social-Democracy, Noske, counter-revolutionary Menshevism, to Stalinism, its economic and social roots at each stage, its political manifestations, its contradictions and antagonisms. Unless Stalinism is attacked as the most potent mode of the counter-revolution, the counter-revolution of our epoch, it cannot be seriously attacked. But once this conception is grasped in *all* its implications, philosophical and methodological, then Stalinism and *its* methods, *its* principles, *its* aims, can be dealt a series of expanding blows against which it has no defense except slander and assassination. Our document gives only a faint outline of the tremendous scope of the revolutionary attack on Stalinism which the theory of state-capitalism opens up. It is the very nature of our age which brings philosophy from Lenin's study in 1914 to the very forefront of the struggle for the remaking of the world.

Orthodox Trotskyism

From all this, the Fourth International has cut itself off by its state-property theory.

The philosophical root of Trotsky's mistake is not new, it is not difficult when fully explained. The categories, the forms established by the proletarian revolution in 1917, he took as permanent, fixed. The October Revolution had undoubtedly manifested itself most strikingly in opposition to bourgeois society by the abolition of private property and the institution of planning in the sense of ability to direct "capital." Trotsky drew the conclusion that this was the distinguishing mark of the proletarian revolution. The reformist bureaucracy was attached to private property, defense of the national state, slavishly served the bourgeoisie, capitulated to it in crisis. He drew the conclusion that all labor bureaucracies in the future would do the same, more or less. The revolutionary party established state-property and was defeatist toward the national state. Hence only revolutionary parties could do the same. Trotsky did not recognize that although the October Revolution took these forms, the forms were not permanent. There were antagonisms within them which would grow and develop with the class struggle, presenting the revolution in new modes. His philosophical method is known and clearly defined by Hegel—the method of synthetic cognition.

Today, the reading of Lenin shows that he never at any time allowed himself to slip from seeing socialism as proletarian *power*, using all necessary and objective forms but carefully distinguishing the *fundamental universal* of proletarian power from the concrete molds into which history had forced that specific revolution. For Lenin *the* readiness of Russia for socialism was the appearance of the Soviet, a new form of social organization.

Trotsky, however, did not see what took place between 1944 and today. He is not in any way responsible for the philosophical methods of Pablo and Germain.

Pablo has simply substituted *degeneration* for the universal of proletarian power. This road is the road to ruin whether by way of Stalinism or otherwise. Lenin's *State and Revolution* is not a "norm." It was the universal drawn from analysis of the class struggle on a world scale and generalized. It was an indispensable necessity of thought, by means of which Lenin could grasp the concrete reality of 1917. Thought is and *must be* a relation between the class, in our case the proletariat, the concrete conditions (Russia in 1917) and the universal. Without the universal of proletarian democracy, as Lenin pointed out with the utmost emphasis in 1916 against the imperialist economists, the bourgeois crisis produces inevitably a "*depression* or *suppression* of human reasoning."

There is only *"the effect* of the horrible impressions, the painful consequences. . . ."* Lenin was not talking psychology. It was, he insisted, the
method of *thought* which was at stake.

In 1950, the universal is as far beyond 1917 as 1917 was beyond
the Paris Commune. A serious analysis of Stalinism will show that it
is precisely the advanced objective relations of society which compel
the counter-revolution to assume this form and dress itself in Marxism,
fake action committees and all. We have to draw a new universal, more
concrete and embracing more creative freedom of the masses than even
State and Revolution.

It is at this time that Pablo not only fails to do so but repudiates *State
and Revolution,* proposing instead that proletarian politics be guided
for centuries by the barbarous degradation in Russia and in the buffer
states of Eastern Europe. It is the end of any philosophic method and
the most serious of all theories of retrogression. In this mentality can be
seen the germs which in maturity make the complete Stalinist—absolute
hostility to capitalism as we have known it but a resigned acceptance
that Marx's and Lenin's ideas of proletarian power are Utopian. No more
deadly deviation has ever appeared in our movement.

Germain has no philosophical method for which we can spare
space and time. He bounces from side to side, affirming theories, drop-
ping them and building new ones, listing innumerable possibilities, analyzing not the laws of capitalism but Outer Mongolia and the decrees of
Mussolini in Northern Italy, gripped in that most terrible of all logics,
the logic of empiricism; effective only in this important sense that his
undisciplined verbiage and shifting generalizations prepare minds for
some such brutal solution as Pablo's.

In a dark time Trotskyism maintained the continuity and struggled
for the essentials of Bolshevism. Its errors are not irreparable. Today it
faces two roads: Pablo's road and the road of "Johnson-Forest." The longer the hesitation, the greater the price that will be paid.

August 4th, 1950

Glossary

Christian Humanism – Neo-conservative philosophy associated with "Corporatist" efforts to reconcile Capital and Labor under the tutelage of the Catholic Church.

Pierre Frank – A leading figure of French Trotskyism.

Germain – 1940s "party name" of Ernest Mandel, leading Trotskyist economic theorist, and the most prominent Belgian Trotskyist.

GPU – The USSR's secret police.

Joseph Hansen – Personal Secretary to Leon Trotsky in Trotsky's final years; later a leading figure in the U.S. Socialist Workers Party and the Fourth International; editor of *International Press Correspondence*.

Pablo [real name: Michel Raptis] – Trotskyist theoretician, best known for his program of abandoning the organization of separate Trotskyist parties and a separate Trotskyist international, in favor of unity with independent-minded Communist movements.

The Revolution Betrayed – Trotsky's 1936 historical interpretation of the rise of Stalin's bureaucracy in Russia.

Stakhanovism – A system of speed-up and stretch-out of Soviet Russian production, after 1935, tying workers' wages to individual output and initiative; named for Alexei Stakhanov, a widely feted coal-miner.

Taylorism – Rationalization of production in U.S. industry, so named after Frederick Taylor, father of the "time-study" method.

Eugen Varga – Prominent Russian economist associated with efforts toward internal reform of the system's various abuses.

Wallace Movement – Followers of Henry Wallace, former Vice-President (under Franklin Delano Roosevelt) who ran for President in 1948 on the Progressive Party ticket, with Communist Party support.

A. Zhdanov – Russian Communist Party leader who became Stalin's principal theorist during the era of mass purges in the 1930s. He later was "retired" by an envious Stalin before expiring under mysterious circumstances.

About
PM Press

politics • culture • art • fiction • music • film

PM Press was founded at the end of 2007 by a small collection of folks with decades of publishing, media, and organizing experience. PM Press co-conspirators have published and distributed hundreds of books, pamphlets, CDs, and DVDs. Members of PM have founded enduring book fairs, spearheaded victorious tenant organizing campaigns, and worked closely with bookstores, academic conferences, and even rock bands to deliver political and challenging ideas to all walks of life. We're old enough to know what we're doing and young enough to know what's at stake.

We seek to create radical and stimulating fiction and nonfiction books, pamphlets, T-shirts, visual and audio materials to entertain, educate, and inspire you. We aim to distribute these through every available channel with every available technology, whether that means you are seeing anarchist classics at our bookfair stalls; reading our latest vegan cookbook at the café; downloading geeky fiction e-books; or digging new music and timely videos from our website.

Contact us for direct ordering and questions about all PM Press releases, as well as manuscript submissions, review copy requests, foreign rights sales, author interviews, to book an author for an event, and to have PM Press attend your bookfair:

PM Press • PO Box 23912 • Oakland, CA 94623
510-658-3906 • info@pmpress.org

Buy books and stay on top of what we are doing at:

www.pmpress.org

A New Notion
Two Works by C.L.R. James:
"Every Cook Can Govern"
and "The Invading Socialist
Society"
C.L.R. James
Edited by Noel Ignatiev
$16.95 • 160 Pages
ISBN: 978-1-60486-047-4

C.L.R. James was a leading figure in the independence movement in the West Indies, and the black and working-class movements in both Britain and the United States. As a major contributor to Marxist and revolutionary theory, his project was to discover, document, and elaborate the aspects of working-class activity that constitute the revolution in today's world. In this volume, Noel Ignatiev, author of *How the Irish Became White*, provides an extensive introduction to James' life and thought, before presenting two critical works that together illustrate the tremendous breadth and depth of James' worldview.

"The Invading Socialist Society," for James the fundamental document of his political tendency, shows clearly the power of James' political acumen and its relevance in today's world with a clarity of analysis that anticipated future events to a remarkable extent. "Every Cook Can Govern," is a short and eminently readable piece counterpoising direct with representative democracy, and getting to the heart of how we should relate to one another. Together these two works represent the principal themes that run through James's life: implacable hostility toward all "condescending saviors" of the working class, and undying faith in the power of ordinary people to build a new world.

A HISTORY OF PAN-AFRICAN REVOLT

C.L.R. James
Introduction by Robin D.G. Kelley
$16.95 • 160 pages
ISBN: 978-1-60486-095-5

Originally published in England in 1938 (the same year as his magnum opus *The Black Jacobins*) and expanded in 1969, this work remains the classic account of global black resistance. Robin D.G. Kelley's substantial introduction contextualizes the work in the history and ferment of the times, and explores its ongoing relevance today.

"*A History of Pan-African Revolt* is one of those rare books that continues to strike a chord of urgency, even half a century after it was first published. Time and time again, its lessons have proven to be valuable and relevant for understanding liberation movements in Africa and the diaspora. Each generation who has had the opportunity to read this small book finds new insights, new lessons, new visions for their own age . . .. No piece of literature can substitute for a crystal ball, and only religious fundamentalists believe that a book can provide comprehensive answers to all questions. But if nothing else, *A History of Pan-African Revolt* leaves us with two incontrovertible facts. First, as long as black people are denied freedom, humanity and a decent standard of living, they will continue to revolt. Second, unless these revolts involve the ordinary masses and take place on their own terms, they have no hope of succeeding."
 —Robin D.G. Kelley, from the Introduction

"I wish my readers to understand the history of Pan-African Revolt. They fought, they suffered—they are still fighting. Once we understand that, we can tackle our problems with the necessary mental equilibrium."
 —C.L.R. James

Modern Politics
C.L.R. James
Introduction by Noel Ignatiev
$16.95 • 176 pages
ISBN: 978-1-60486-311-6

"Marxists envisage a total change in the basic structure of human relations. With that change our problems will not be solved overnight, but we will be able to tackle them with confidence. Such are the difficulties, contradictions, and antagonisms; and in the solution of them society moves forward and men and women feel they have a role in the development of their social surroundings. It is in this movement that we have the possibility of a good life."
    —C.L.R. James, from *Modern Politics*

This volume provides a brilliant and accessible summation of the ideas of left Marxist giant C.L.R. James. Originally delivered in 1960 as a series of lectures in his native Trinidad, these writings powerfully display his wide-ranging erudition and enduring relevance. From his analysis of revolutionary history (from the Athenian city-states through the English Revolution, Russian Revolution, and the Hungarian Revolution of 1956), to the role of literature, art, and culture in society (from Charlie Chaplin to Pablo Picasso, via Camus and Einstein), to an interrogation of the ideas and philosophy of such thinkers as Rousseau, Lenin, and Trotsky, this is a magnificent tour de force from a critically engaged thinker at the height of his powers. An essential introduction to a body of work as necessary and illuminating for this century as it proved for the last.

FOPM

MONTHLY SUBSCRIPTION PROGRAM

These are indisputably momentous times—the financial system is melting down globally and the Empire is stumbling. Now more than ever there is a vital need for radical ideas.

In the six years since its founding—and on a mere shoestring—PM Press has risen to the formidable challenge of publishing and distributing knowledge and entertainment for the struggles ahead. With over 250 releases to date, we have published an impressive and stimulating array of literature, art, music, politics, and culture. Using every available medium, we've succeeded in connecting those hungry for ideas and information to those putting them into practice.

Friends of PM allows you to directly help impact, amplify, and revitalize the discourse and actions of radical writers, filmmakers, and artists. It provides us with a stable foundation from which we can build upon our early successes and provides a much-needed subsidy for the materials that can't necessarily pay their own way. You can help make that happen—and receive every new title automatically delivered to your door once a month—by joining as a Friend of PM Press. And, we'll throw in a free T-shirt when you sign up.

Here are your options:

- $30 a month: Get all books and pamphlets plus 50% discount on all webstore purchases
- $40 a month: Get all PM Press releases (including CDs and DVDs) plus 50% discount on all webstore purchases
- $100 a month: Superstar—Everything plus PM merchandise, free downloads, and 50% discount on all webstore purchases

For those who can't afford $30 or more a month, we're introducing **Sustainer Rates** at $15, $10 and $5. Sustainers get a free PM Press T-shirt and a 50% discount on all purchases from our website.

Your Visa or Mastercard will be billed once a month, until you tell us to stop. Or until our efforts succeed in bringing the revolution around. Or the financial meltdown of Capital makes plastic redundant. Whichever comes first.

CPSIA information can be obtained
at www.ICGtesting.com
Printed in the USA
JSHW010708030922
29975JS00003B/3